W. D. HOWELLS,
TRAVELER FROM ALTRURIA

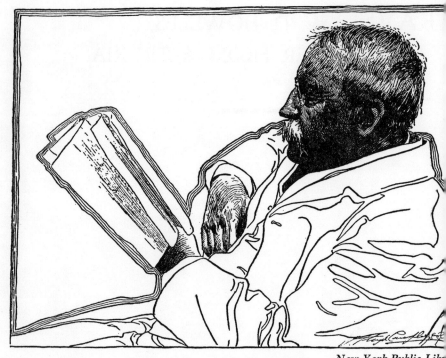

Sketch of W. D. Howells by Floyd Campbell from *Book-lovers*, December, 1903, after a photograph by Zaida Ben-Yusuf in *The Critic*, November, 1897

W. D. HOWELLS,
TRAVELER FROM ALTRURIA
1889-1894

by

CLARA MARBURG KIRK

RUTGERS UNIVERSITY PRESS

New Brunswick   *New Jersey*

TO RUDOLF

Fellow Traveler in Altruria

"What is this hanging here? A map of Altruria? It is an outlandish region inhabited by people of heart, a sort of economic Pays du Tendre. It ought not to be tolerated; and yet I traversed parts of it in my *Little Journey in the World*, and the inhabitants, though not much better than early Christian socialists, seem to mean well. Leave the map for a while!"

"Editors Study," *Harper's Monthly*, March, 1892

Preface

The chance reading of an editorial on William Dean Howells in the *Brooklyn Daily Eagle* of May 11, 1920, marked the beginning of a trail that finally has led to the present study. A few hours after he had heard the news of Howells' death, the unidentified editorial writer said of "our leading novelist": "He called himself a Socialist, he joined the Church of the Carpenter in Boston in an effort to exalt the life of Jesus above the creeds of the churches, and he signed the appeal for the pardon of the Chicago anarchists, but his was not the spirit of a crusader."

In an effort to sift truth from untruth in this statement, Rudolf Kirk and I set out on a search that led us from the New York Public Library to the Houghton Collection at Harvard, to the Library of Congress—to mention only a few of the reading rooms we haunted. The new material we uncovered on Howells' connection with the Church of the Carpenter from 1889 to 1894 we summarized in an article for the *New England Quarterly* (June, 1959), with the full realization that much remained unsaid. In 1961 we welcomed the opportunity to publish Howells' *Letters of an Altrurian Traveller* (Scholars' Facsimile and Reprints) on the same subject. These previously uncollected letters supply the link between *A Traveler From Altruria* * (1894)

* Howells' spelling of "Traveler" was not consistent; he spelt the word with two *l*'s when the essays appeared in *The Cosmo-*

and *Through the Eye of the Needle* (1907), and must be considered in further studies of Howells' liberal thought in the 1890's.

But to sort out the documents is not to answer the questions raised by the editorial in the *Brooklyn Daily Eagle*. Was Howells a Socialist? Was he, indeed, a Christian? Or a "crusader"? After two years in Boston (1889–1891), when he was associated with members of the Church of the Carpenter, the Nationalist Club, and other liberal groups, Howells returned to New York to edit, for a brief time, *The Cosmopolitan*, in which he published two series of Altrurian essays. In these urbanely ironic but sharply critical conversations and letters, Howells himself—faintly disguised as a traveler from an imaginary Grecian island—suggested the answers to the teasing questions proposed in the editorial after his death.

The present study is, in a sense, an interpretation of Howells' view of the American scene between 1889 and 1894, as seen through the eyes of a Christianized Greek traveler; it is, at the same time, a study of the people Howells met in editorial offices and at dinner parties, of the books he happened to be reading during those years, and of his relation to the magazines in which he hoped to publish. No studies of Howells' "ideas" can be made in a vacuum, for they always prove to be an aspect of his biography; what Howells thought always grew out of what he was experiencing at any given period.

Many scholars, of course, have considered Howells' social attitudes of the periods before and after these five

politan, and with one *l* when it was used in the title, *A Traveler From Altruria* (1894). Throughout this book the latter spelling is used except when "Traveller" occurs in a title. (See also Note 10 to Chapter IV.)

years. George Arms's "The Literary Background of Howells's Social Criticism" (*American Literature*, November,
1942) first enlarged my thoughts on the subject. Since then
William M. Gibson, Everett Carter, Louis J. Budd, Edwin
H. Cady, John Reeves, and others have written suggestively
on various aspects of Howells' social development in the
1880's and 1890's. In the "complicity" of the thinking of
these scholars, I am unable to unravel my own indebtedness.
I should like, however, to acknowledge a particular obligation to Rudolf Kirk, who has not only read the manuscript
several times but also has supplied much of the material;
to George Arms, whose wide knowledge of Howells I have
relied on for years; to the Rutgers Research Council, which
has made possible the publication of this book. I wish also
to thank Miss Mildred Howells, Professor W. W. Howells,
and the Houghton Library of Harvard University for permission to quote from Howells' published and unpublished
writing. No one may use these quotations without their
specific consent.

CLARA MARBURG KIRK

Douglass College
Rutgers, The State University
January, 1962

Contents

Contents

W. D. HOWELLS,
TRAVELER FROM ALTRURIA

Introduction

William Dean Howells introduced Aristides Homos, Traveler from Altruria, to his readers early in the 1890's, at a time when he himself was deeply concerned over the social evils of a rapidly industrializing country. Several years earlier he had written his friend Henry James, "I'm not in a very good humor with 'America' myself"; and he added, "I should hardly like to trust pen and ink with all the audacity of my social ideas; but after fifty years of optimistic content with 'civilization' and its ability to come out all right in the end, I now abhor it, and feel that it is coming out all wrong in the end, unless it bases itself anew on a real equality." [1] No longer convinced that "the more smiling aspects of life" were "the more American," Howells was at that time seeking for the proper medium for his social ideas. Clearly they seemed to him too potent for his annual novel, or, indeed, for the columns of the "Editor's Study," in which he was then expressing his views each month in *Harper's Monthly Magazine*.

In the November, 1892, issue of *The Cosmopolitan*, Mr. Homos, a traveler from Altruria, made his appearance, as the guest of a dapper and successful novelist, Mr. Twelvemough, whom one immediately recognizes as Howells himself, in his more conventional aspects, as a writer of serial novels for popular magazines. Mr. Homos, from the moment he stepped off his train in a New Hampshire summer resort, was a puzzle and a bother to his host for the very reason that he seemed to live according to the concepts of "a real equality" practiced in "Altruria," the imaginary homeland with which Howells had provided him, and thus to offend at every turn the undemocratic customs of "Egoria," the name Howells gave to America. Mr. Twelvemough found Mr. Homos very attractive and could not "look upon his face without feeling a glow of kindness for him," in spite of the fact that the Altrurian had "no manners." Would a true gentleman, for instance, insist on carrying his own luggage? He tended further to confuse his host by his outspoken "ideas," frequently expressed in the form of seemingly simple questions, such as, "No social slight attaches to service, I suppose?" Why should the popular Mr. Twelvemough, whose novels, like those of Howells, appeared annually in neat little duodecimo volumes,[2] be challenged by this naïve and tiresome stranger with such trivial questions as those suggested by the services of a baggage carrier? How much more attractive to novel readers generally were the "April Hopes" (to borrow the title of one of Howells' recent novels) engendered in a youthful heart at a Harvard tea party, for example? Try as he might to turn away from the implications of his guest's innocent questions, Mr. Twelvemough was unable to do so, for, indeed, as the reader slowly realizes, Mr. Homos and Mr. Twelvemough are two sides of Howells himself.

In the characters of Mr. Homos and Mr. Twelvemough, Howells thus found an indirect way of dramatizing his own conflict of ideas. At this time Howells' concern with social problems actually threatened his interest in novel-writing, and in his Altrurian essays he attempted to resolve his conflict. The setting he chose for his discussions of "conditions in America" in the summer of 1892 was the wide piazza of a mountain hotel; the other characters, representing different aspects of our national life, were a banker, a minister, a doctor, a lawyer, and a professor, as well as a scattering of country folk, society ladies, and casual summer guests.

After an uncomfortable dinner, in the course of which the Traveler attempted to help the pretty schoolteacher-waitress to carry her heavy tray, Mr. Twelvemough was glad to turn over his difficult guest to the gentlemen enjoying their after-dinner cigars on the verandah. "Mr. Homos is from Altruria," he explained; "he is visiting our country for the first time, and is greatly interested in the working of our institutions. He has been asking me some rather hard questions about certain phases of our civilization; and the fact is that I have launched him upon you because I don't feel quite able to cope with him." Mr. Twelvemough, the imaginary author of "Glove and Gauntlet" and "Airs and Graces," was no more competent to cope with the "audacity of [the] social ideas" of Mr. Homos than Howells felt able to deal with his own when he wrote to James in 1888. Nor, indeed, were the other gentlemen on the hotel porch, in spite of their apparent complacency, actually able to answer their visitor's questions. These ranged from the use of strikes as a weapon by labor, to the function of the hotel porter; from the true value of money, to the American custom of tipping; from the problem of the deforested New Hampshire countryside, to the attitude of the summer visitors toward the farmers who supplied their food. Though no one on the porch that summer evening would admit to any uneasiness, all were vaguely apprehensive, for the United States in 1892 was rapidly moving toward the worst depression the country had known for twenty years, and the signs were not difficult to read. Increased poverty,

strikes, unemployment, high tariff, and tight money affected the lives of summer guests and country hosts as well.
The questions raised by the Traveler were those asked on
all sides during the Presidential campaign, then raging, that
in 1892 sent Cleveland to the White House for his second
term. But before the Altrurian had an opportunity to for-
mulate his questions concerning Egoria, the group of Americans glanced at him with polite curiosity and asked several
questions of their own about the little-known land from
which he had come.

"Is it long since you left Altruria?" asked the banker,
Mr. Bullion, opening the way to further conversation by
gently prodding the stranger as to his identity. The Altrurian's rather guarded reply—"It seems a great while ago,
but it is really only a few weeks"—and the inquiries that
followed must be heard before we consider the range of the
ideas the Traveler brought from his far-off land, distant in
time as well as in space.

" 'You came by way of England, I suppose?' "

" 'Yes; there is no direct line to America,' " responded
their guest.

But the professor in the group was not satisfied with this
simple explanation of the origin of the Altrurian.

" 'Your name is Greek, isn't it, Mr. Homos?' " he in-
quired innocently.

" 'Yes; we are of one of the early Hellenic families,' "
replied the stranger.

The lawyer, who was, like most lawyers, "a lover of
romance" and "well read in legendary lore," asked Mr.
Homos whether there was any reason for identifying Altruria with "the fabled Atlantis."

" 'No,' " the Traveler replied; no such tradition existed.
" 'Besides,' " he continued, "our civilization is strictly

Christian, and dates back to no earlier period than that of the first Christian commune after Christ."

The Altrurian's next remark, and the last reference he made to the history of his country, made clear to the reader that Altruria lay directly on the route from Palestine to England, over which Christianity, modified by Greek philosophy, was carried to the West: "It is a matter of history with us that one of these communists when [the early Christians] were dispersed, brought the gospel to our continent; he was cast away on our eastern coast on his way to Britain."

Though Altruria might seem remote from America, the Traveler explained, it was actually nearer to this country than most people realized—it was, in fact, "only a thought away." Bemused by the possible implications of their guest's remarks, the questioners remained silent for a moment, thoughtfully puffing their cigars. Then the minister, the most literal-minded member of the circle, remarked softly, "It is perfectly astonishing that an island so large as Altruria should have been lost to the knowledge of the rest of the world ever since the beginning of our era." [3]

The minister expressed Howells' own mock wonderment that Altruria, where the Greek and Christian world converged, should have been forgotten by Americans, whose national culture was founded on the concepts of these two great civilizations. Homos hardly comprehended the minister's remarks, for he did not at first realize that Americans had forgotten their own basic documents. He was delighted to find himself in a country that affirmed "the essential equality of man," as set forth in "your glorious Declaration." Mr. Twelvemough asked in surprise, "Ah, you have read our Declaration of Independence then?" His visitor replied, "Every Altrurian has read that." [4] Because the

Traveler had not become inured to the fact that Americans, in their daily intercourse, by no means reflected a belief in the equality of man, he was guilty of a series of social blunders in his efforts to share the work-burden of waitresses and baggage men. Apologizing to his chagrined host, he said, "You must excuse the confusion which the difference between your political ideals and your economic ideals constantly creates in me. . . . It is very puzzling." [5]

It soon became apparent to the novelist, as well as to all the other gentlemen conversing with Aristides Homos on the porch of the summer hotel, that their guest was taking literally a document which sensible men had tacitly agreed to disregard. Mr. Bullion, the most articulate member of the group, attempted to explain to Homos that "business" had become our "national ideal," that we were no longer distracted by eighteenth-century political notions of equality: "This is a business man's country. We are a purely commercial people; money is absolutely to the fore; and business, which is the means of getting the most money, is the American ideal." [6]

The banker's assertion did not go unchallenged; the lawyer, the professor, the minister, the doctor, all commented, pondered, argued as the night wore on. At last it occurred to the company that it might be interesting to persuade the Altrurian "to open up about his native land," which, he told them, "emerged from the competitive conditions . . . many hundred years ago." [7] Like Egoria (where egoism then held sway) the Traveler's homeland (where altruism prevailed) had passed through a fiercely competitive period, known as the Age of Accumulation. Egoria eventually will become Altruria, after a period of fruitless strife, quietly observed the Altrurian, for "the difference between your civilization and ours is only one of degree after all. . . . America and Altruria are really one at heart." [8]

When, a few days later, the Altrurian, in a lengthy speech to the whole community, attempted to give "a clear account of the present state of things in my country," he began with the story of Paul's bringing Christianity to the Greeks. "The apostle cast away upon our heathen coasts, won us with the story of this first Christian republic, and he established a commonwealth of peace and goodwill among us in its likeness." However, the Altrurian told his audience, this commonwealth perished, as did others after it; "long ages of civic and economic warfare succeeded, when every man's hand was against his neighbor, and might was the rule that got itself called right." Religion lost its potency as a guide in this world and became nothing more than "the vague promise of the next. We descended into the valley of the shadow, and dwelt amid chaos for ages, before we groped again into the light." [9] It is like a waking dream to find oneself, he said, in the presence of conditions here that Altrurians outlived so long ago.

With this thinly disguised allegory of the "plutocracy" of the United States in 1892, when "the love of money . . . was filling the earth with the hate of men," Howells presented his interpretation of the political and economic confusion and corruption of the 1890's in the twelve essays he wrote for *The Cosmopolitan* soon after his two years in Boston (1889–1891), where his association with an active group of Christian Socialists had focused his restless dissatisfaction with "plutocratic" America. A chance rereading of Goldsmith's *History of Greece* on his return to New York suggested to Howells a form for the expression of the "audacity of [his] social ideas." The result was the publication of "A Traveller From Altruria" in the recently revived *Cosmopolitan*, which he had agreed to edit. Before these essays appeared in book form in 1894, Howells was well launched on a second series of eleven "Letters of an Altrurian Traveler," which came to a close in 1894. Between the appearance of the first and the last of the Altrurian essays in *The Cosmopolitan*, November, 1892, and October, 1894, the country had moved into a depression that lasted through the decade. Never in sympathy with President Cleveland, Howells became increasingly aware of the growing power of the industrial East at the expense of the agricultural West and South. Though he was unwilling to commit himself publicly, Howells' essays in this period reflected his social views, which were sympathetic with industrial and agrarian workers and were closely related to those of the new Populist Party. Since Howells' social and political leanings at this period in his life are of particular interest, we shall in the following study discuss in some detail the twenty-three essays that Howells wrote for *The Cosmopolitan* early in the 1890's. We shall glance only briefly at the two later additions to his Altrurian series in *Through the Eye of the Needle* (1907), for these are the less important expressions of the disillusionment of an elderly idealist.

Soon after the appearance of *A Traveler From Altruria* in book form, a brief article appeared in the July 4, 1896, issue of *Harper's Weekly*,[10] under a handsome engraving of Howells, which reported that during the serializing of *A Traveler*, the author received "more letters about it than about any other story he had written in many and many a year—'letters from all over the country and from all kinds of people.'" Howells further remarked that the book was an answer to the "grave questions" which had arisen in his mind at that time, that it was a "partial solution" to problems which confronted him and refused to be easily dismissed. These disturbing questions grew out of the experiences that came to Howells between 1889 and 1894 and caused him to reflect upon our American civilization; his "partial solution," reflected in *A Traveler*, is important to an understanding of his more serious contributions as a novelist during these years.

Howells identified himself with the Traveler from Altruria, the stranger who had come from an island where the Christian and the Classical worlds had mingled their best ideas on the "real equality" of men; through the eyes of the Altrurian, Howells suddenly saw the shortcomings of his fellow citizens of Egoria. America, having evolved into a wealthy, competitive state, must return, Howells maintained, to "the truer state" defined by the Declaration of Independence, at a time when a Christian belief in the common man was fused with a Greek respect for civil liberties. By means of his twenty-five Altrurian essays, Howells wished to lead his countrymen "into the light" shed by our double tradition and away from the "civic and economic warfare" which he saw about him. But, as we have suggested, Howells was Mr. Twelvemough as well as Mr. Homos; until he had imagined for himself this dual role of popular novelist and ardent reformer, he could not "trust pen and ink" with the boldness of his thoughts on America. The novelist and the social critic, both of whom dwelt in Howells, were not in perfect harmony with each other, though they professed to be friends. Turning to Mr. Twelvemough, Mr. Homos had smilingly observed to the other Americans present, "I have fancied in my friend here, a suspicion that I was not entirely single in some of the inquiries I have made, but that I had some ulterior motive, some wish to censure or satirize." Mr. Twelvemough, too polite to admit such an accurate conjecture, had protested, "Oh, not at all! We are so well satisfied with our condition that we have nothing but pity for the darkened mind of the foreigner." [11] Urbane good manners and an underlying play of ironic amusement held the argument in bounds throughout these essays, but the conflict within Howells' mind was intense and even painful.

When Howells composed his farewell paper for the "Editor's Study" in March, 1892, Mr. Homos was clearly in the ascendency. As Howells packed away the plaster busts of his discredited favorites, Tolstoy, Ibsen, Zola, and the rest, which had adorned his shelves, the eyes of the retiring editor fell upon a map of Altruria hanging on the wall of his study. Like Mr. Twelvemough, Howells considered Altruria "an outlandish region" that really "ought not to be tolerated," but like Mr. Homos, he thought the map reminiscent of an ancient "carte" of the "Pays du Tendre" [12] that directed the traveler to follow the "River of Inclination," past the "Rock of Pride" and the "Sea of Enmity," to "Countrys Undiscovered." "I traversed part of it in my *Little Journey in the World*," [13] Howells mused; he had discovered that the inhabitants meant very well, and that they were, indeed, not unlike the Christian Socialists he had come to know in Boston. "Leave the map for a while!" he said, as he softly closed the door.

NOTES

"A Traveller From Altruria" first appeared in twelve issues of *The Cosmopolitan*, XIV–XV, November, 1892–October, 1893. Eleven "Letters of an Altrurian Traveller" appeared in *The Cos-*

mopolitan, XVI–XVII, November, 1893–September, 1894. The first two "Letters" were not reprinted during Howells' lifetime. The next three essays of this series were contracted into two essays in *Impressions and Experiences* (1896); the remaining six "Letters" were made into Part One of *Through the Eye of the Needle* (1907). These eleven "Letters," as they appeared originally, have been gathered together in *Letters of an Altrurian Traveller*, edited by Clara M. Kirk and Rudolf Kirk (Scholars' Facsimile and Reprints, 1961).

Citations to texts in this study are, first, to the essays as they came out in *The Cosmopolitan*, and then to their first appearance in book form. Because of the complexity of the textual question involved, a double reference seems desirable. Hereafter, *A Traveler From Altruria* (1894) will be referred to as *A Traveler*, and *The Letters of an Altrurian Traveller* (1961) will be referred to as *The Letters*.

1. Howells to James, October 10, 1888. *Life in Letters of William Dean Howells* (2 vols.) edited by Mildred Howells (1928), I, 417.

2. In the language of printers, the word is written "twelvemo," referring to duodecimo volumes. Apparently Howells himself altered the spelling to "Twelvemough."

3. "A Traveller From Altruria," *The Cosmopolitan*, XIV (January, 1893), 341–342. *A Traveler*, pp. 46–48. For further information on "altruism" in this country, see "Altruism Arrives in America," Louis J. Budd, *American Quarterly* VIII (Spring, 1956), 40–52. Budd makes it clear that the concept of "altruism" was popular in the last quarter of the nineteenth century in this country. Auguste Comte first used the word "altruism" in his *System of Positive Polity* (1851–1854); Howells invented the term "Altruria" to designate the mythical island where altruism flourishes.

4. *The Cosmopolitan*, XIV (November, 1892), 55. *A Traveler*, p. 12.

5. *The Cosmopolitan*, XIV (March, 1893), 635. *A Traveler*, p. 98.

6. *The Cosmopolitan*, XV (July, 1893), 306. *A Traveler*, pp. 214–215.

7. *The Cosmopolitan*, p. 310. *A Traveler*, p. 229.

8. *The Cosmopolitan*, XIV (December, 1892), 253. *A Traveler*, p. 31.

9. *The Cosmopolitan*, XV (September, 1893), 635. *A Traveler*, p. 257.
10. Marrion Wilcox, "Works of William Dean Howells," *Harper's Weekly*, XL (July 4, 1896), 656. The engraving was made from a photograph by G. C. Cox.
11. *The Cosmopolitan*, XIV (January, 1893), 342. *A Traveler*, p. 49.
12. For a reproduction of a map of the "Pays du Tendre" (1678), see *The English Novel in the Time of Shakespeare*, J. J. Jusserand (London, 1890), p. 359.
13. *Little Journey in the World*, Charles Dudley Warner (1889).

Chapter I

Christian Socialism
Boston, 1889–1891

Soon after Howells assumed his duties on *Harper's Magazine* (January, 1886) he read for the first time a story by Tolstoy, *The Cossacks*, which had been in his possession, though unread, for some time. Later, in looking back over this period in his life, Howells wrote that no writer had so profoundly modified his way of thinking as had Tolstoy; that, indeed, he could "never again see life" in the way he saw it before he came in contact with the thought of the great Christian Socialist of Russia, who gave him "heart to hope that the world may yet be made over in the image of Him who died for it." [1] After reading *The Cossacks*, Howells turned to Tolstoy's essays, *My Religion* and *Scenes of the Siege of Sebastopol*, which he promptly reviewed in the "Editor's Study" of April, 1886.

Just one month after the appearance of Howells' review of Tolstoy's essays, news was flashed across the country of a mass meeting held, on May 4, 1886, in Haymarket Square, Chicago, of strikers for an eight-hour day, which culminated in the throwing of a bomb that killed several policemen and wounded a number of bystanders. Troops were at once summoned and strikers in the crowd were arrested, not so much because there was any evidence against them as that they were thought to be connected with loosely-defined groups of "anarchists" then troubling Chicago. Howells, like many another concerned American, followed the unfolding story of the "Chicago Anarchists" as it was reported in the newspapers, and thus became increasingly aware of the deep-seated social struggle in the country, dramatically highlighted by the bloody strife of May, 1886.

While this public debate was still front-page news, a translation of Tolstoy's *Que Faire?* (*What Shall We Do About It?*) appeared in this country. Howells immediately reviewed it in the "Editor's Study," July, 1887. "The terrible, unsparing honesty" of Tolstoy, that "singular Russian nobleman," suggested to Howells a social philosophy which permanently affected his thinking. Not only Howells, but also social theorists such as Richard T. Ely, Henry George, and Edward Bellamy, were deeply moved by Tolstoy's essay. Addressed, as Howells pointed out in his review, to all "sinners and sufferers" like himself, *Que Faire?* almost immediately became a kind of handbook for the rapidly growing movement of Christian Socialism. The events resulting from the disturbance in Chicago swept Howells into this movement into which many of his friends had already been drawn.

After a year of bitter public discussion of the tragedy, the Supreme Court on November 2, 1887, confirmed the conviction of the eight men accused of the death of the policemen. Howells, at the risk of his position with *Harper's*, immediately wrote a letter to the *New York Tribune*, November 6, 1887, in a last-minute effort to save the condemned men. In his letter appealing for clemency, Howells urged his readers to petition Governor Altgeld of Illinois to commute the death penalty of the accused to life imprisonment. Howells' prompt and dramatic response to these national events must have been deeply influenced by the impact of Tolstoy's thoughts which had recently seized upon his imagination and seemed to awaken in him fresh concepts of the real meaning of "the brotherhood of man." When, the following week, four of the eight "Chicago Anarchists" were hanged, Howells suffered a shock at what seemed to him a tragic miscarriage of justice, from which he never wholly recovered. On November 18, 1887, he wrote his sister in Ohio that he and his wife no longer cared for "the world's life, and would like to settle somewhere very humbly and simply, where we could be socially identified with the principles of progress and sympathy for the struggling mass." The last two months, he wrote, "have been full of heartache and horror," because of the "civic murder committed last Friday at Chicago." The accused men were "unfairly tried and most unjustly condemned. . . . It's all been an atrocious piece of frenzy and cruelty, for which we must stand ashamed forever before history. But it's no use. I can't write about it. Some day I hope to do justice to these irreparably wronged men." [2]

J. W. Harper, then head of the House of Harper, made no objection to Howells' letter to the *Tribune*, though, as Howells recorded many years later, "I suppose it was as distasteful to the House as it was to the immeasurable majority of the American people." [3] Howells had not condoned the use of violence by the strikers in Chicago's Haymarket Square; he had, however, protested the conviction of the anarchists on insufficient evidence. This distinction Harper understood, and, as an experienced publisher, he realized, too, that Howells had gained in his standing as a writer by his clear and selfless appeal for justice.

An unpublished letter from the editor of *Harper's*, Henry Mills Alden, to Howells, makes clear the publishers' mounting appreciation of the power of the novelist attached to the House. Though no mention is made of the Haymarket affair, Harper's confidence in Howells, as reported by Alden, is apparent. It clearly shows that the publishers and editor of *Harper's* regarded Howells as the writer who had caught the attention of the public by his bold social stand in favor of the Chicago Anarchists and that he was now looked upon as the very man to attract and hold the readers of *Harper's Weekly*, after the excitement of the Cleveland-Harrison Presidential campaign had subsided. The letter is of further interest, for in it J. W. Harper refers to "Howells's sympathy, his altruism—in other words, his warm democratic heart," thus supplying to Howells' sensitive imagination the word "altruism," that he was later to make use of in many essays on the subject. "My dear Howells," wrote Alden, from the editorial room of Harper & Brothers, September 14, 1888,[4]

> You will remember many talks we have had about a series of sketches of New York life. It is an idea in which both Mr. Joseph W. Harper, Jr. & Mr. J. Henry Harper have had, from the first, a lively interest; and it is the same kind of interest which first inclined your heart to the subject—one based on the social meaning of such sketches. The idea occurs to us now with peculiar force as the time approaches for your return to New York, and especially in connection with our *Weekly*. The excitement of the political campaign will soon be over, when the readers of the *Weekly* will turn with fresh zest to a really interesting literary work. But it needs something very strong and very striking to take the place of an absorbing political issue. In this emergency there is no better name to charm with than yours, & no better subject than the one I am recalling to your

attention & which has already engaged so much of your thought.

Mr. Joseph W. Harper, Jr., writing to us from Saratoga, says: "I'm quite sure that we could enlist Howells's sympathy, his altruism—in other words, his warm democratic heart in the preparation of a *feuilleton* for the *Weekly* which would be a powerful presentation of the life of our great metropolis, social, educational, economical, political—as shown in our schools, colleges, charitable organizations, reformatory institutions, prisons, courts of law, occupations & amusements—our streets & parks & factories & clubs—the rich & the poor, the idler & the worker, the silly men & bad men & frivolous women—the elevated railroads, the monopolies, the nuisances—& Hunter's Point.

"Possibly lessons might be drawn from these observations, showing the real assimilation of interests in these diverse classes & occupations of the community, with suggestions for the improvement of society, with the conclusion that one man is as good as another & 'a good deal better, too.' But I should not make this the avowed object of the series—for the avowal would deter readers. When the 'sights of New York' have been dramatically shown from week to week, the reader will 'catch on,' & be prepared for the writer's conclusions, which, indeed, he will anticipate. The *synthetic* plan is the sympathetic plan. When the teacher has dazzled his class with the results of a brilliant experiment, curiosity is stimulated, & his admiring youngsters are prepared for the reason of the thing & eager to know the principle of it.

"Such a series by Howells would command the interest of all classes, afford food for reflection & conversation in society, & would be largely quoted."

I have nothing to add to Mr. Harper's expression of his feeling & opinion, except to say that my disappointment in losing your work for a time in the *Magazine* would be alleviated by the consideration of the great value of such a series to the *Weekly*—a series so timely & so suitable to that periodical.

If you will do this for the *Weekly*, we shall want to make a strong point of it in the announcements of next year's work soon to be sent forth. We wish to hear from you about it at your earliest convenience. The series ought to begin the first week in January, 1889.

In the meantime whatever you do, before you come to New York, in the way of completing any of the short stories you had in mind, will come "handy" to our use.

Yours faithfully,
H. M. Alden

Something of the seriousness of purpose of Howells' outlook during the autumn of 1888 is reflected in a letter he wrote on October 28 to his Boston friend, Edward Everett Hale, a little over a month after he had received the long communication from Alden, carrying with it an invitation to undertake a series of avowedly social sketches of an "altruistic" tone. Howells, in his letter, thanked Hale for sending him several of his novels, and commented on what he thought Hale was accomplishing by his writing:

It is work that no one else can do, and it teaches me patience with conditions that I believe wrong, but that must be borne, with all the possible alleviations, till they can be very gradually changed. I do not think there is any fixed hope of justice under them, but then I know from myself—my own prejudices, passions, follies—that they cannot be bettered except through the unselfishness you enjoin, the immediate altruism dealing with what now is. I know this, while I am persuaded also that the best that is in men, most men, cannot come out till they all have a fair chance. I used to think that America gave this; now I don't.

Not only was Howells disillusioned about the country during this painful year, but he was also dissatisfied with himself. Sociable, humorous, indeed, and often gay by nature, Howells was also tinged with melancholy and self-mistrust; at this time he wrote Hale, "I am neither an example nor an incentive, meanwhile, in my own way of living; I am a creature of the past; only I do believe that I see the light of the future, and that it is this which shows me my ugliness and fatuity and feebleness." But such remarks, he added, are only "Words, words, words! How to make them things, deeds—you have the secret of that; with me they only breed more words." At present, he noted more cheerfully, these words "are running into another novel, in which I'm going to deal with some mere actualities; but on new ground—New York, namely; though I take some characters on from Boston with me." The novel was *A Hazard of New Fortunes*, which Harper had suggested to him the month before; the characters from Boston were Basil and Isabel March, well known to readers of *Their Wedding Journey;* the background was New York, where Howells moved his family a week after he mailed his letter to Hale. "Look me up," Howells wrote at the close of his letter; "I am to be found at 330 East 17th Street." [5]

Though Howells longed, as he supposed, to express his social views in "deeds" rather than in "words," writing was his natural medium then as always; in his apartment high above Stuyvesant Square in New York, Howells began to work in earnest on the novel that helped him to bear his growing awareness of social problems. A brief article in the *Chicago Tribune*, November 12, 1888, reporting a meeting held in Boston the day before, reminds us that there was at least one "deed" which lay at that time within his power to perform, and from which he had withdrawn. No doubt Howells was glad to be in New York, where he could read about the meeting without being present. The article is headed "A Letter From W. D. Howells" and states:

Boston, Nov. 11 (Special).—The Anarchist memorial service in New Era Hall to-night was attended by all who could get into the hall, probably 400. Red flags and mottoes decorated the walls, and though the proceedings were orderly, they were exceedingly noisy by reason of the applause which greeted the speakers. A letter of sympathy was read from W. D. Howells, who briefly reiterated his well-known views that the execution of Spies and his companions was an outrage.

On November 13, 1888, H. M. Alden wrote to Howells requesting permission to state the "facts," lest Howells' position be misunderstood. As a result, *Harper's Weekly* (November 24, 1888) reprinted the letter from Howells to the Committee of Arrangements, and pointed out that it was actually merely a polite note, declining the invitation to speak at the meeting. "I am not a public speaker," Howells had written to the chairman, on November 3, 1888, "and what I had to say of the tragedy of November 11th [1887] I said in my letter printed in the New York Tribune last year, while there was still some hope of saving the victims' lives."

Though Howells did not wish to speak publicly concerning this tragic episode in our history, his December, 1888, "Study" in *Harper's Monthly* bears eloquent witness to the somber tone of his thought at this time, and indicates also how his reading of Tolstoy had colored his outlook. His "Study" is supposedly concerned with Christmas books; however, it is actually a statement of Howells' growing awareness, gained through reading Tolstoy and others, of the possible meaning of Christianity for that period, marked by an increasing disparity between rich and poor. To quote the sober words of the usually ironic editor, "The New Testament . . . is the direct inspiration of the new Christmas literature," especially is it the inspiration of several books by Tolstoy, which Howells proposed to review for the December issue of *Harper's*.

The whole of the testimony [of the work of Tolstoy] is against the system by which a few men win wealth and miserably waste it in idleness and luxury, and the vast mass of men are overworked and underfed. From the volume called *What to Do* [*Que Faire?*], dealing with the poor of Moscow, to the latest utterance from his seclusion—which he calls *Life*, and in which he rises to the question of how a man shall save his soul—he bears perpetual witness against the life that Christendom is now living—the life that seeks the phantom of personal happiness, and ignores the fact that there is and can be no happiness but in the sacrifice of self for others. . . . Christ and the life of Christ is at this moment inspiring the literature of the world as never before.[6]

Concerned as Howells was with the social questions to which he could find no answer, his deepest grief during the early months of the New Year was caused by the illness of his daughter Winifred, who died March 3, 1889. Reflecting on this period many years later, Howells remembered that when he began to write *A Hazard of New Fortunes* during the hopeless illness of his daughter, "I reeled about in it, for I had to write it while the heaviest sorrow I had known was a staggering load on heart and brain." But because he was dealing with social problems of increasing concern to him, he found that the process of writing was in itself restoring. "When I had struggled up, and found my footing," he added, "I believe I went forward with no uncertain tread."[7] Leaving New York in the early summer and moving to New England for two years helped Howells to find his "footing" at a different level.

After a summer at Saratoga, Howells established his home in Boston, at 184 Commonwealth Avenue, where he remained from December, 1889, to December, 1891. His

thoughts, both personal and social, were enlarged and deep-
ened during these years by his association with the Christian Socialists of Boston, which included such well-known
people as Edward Bellamy, Hamlin Garland, Richard T.
Ely, W. D. P. Bliss, Vida Scudder, and other social reform-
ers who were also preachers, teachers, and writers of distinction. This same group—and Howells among them—was
interested in the Nationalist movement, then forming in
Boston. "The Christian Socialists are more to my mind
than the Nationalists," Howells wrote to his father, William
Cooper Howells, on April 27, 1890, adding, characteristi-
cally, "but I doubt if I shall openly act with either for the
present." [8]

The most obvious immediate effect of the rush of new
ideas from this galaxy of associates was political. A Republican of the old abolitionist days, Howells suddenly found
that in the new era of labor unrest his earlier affiliations
were entirely inappropriate to altered conditions. The fact
that the Christian Socialists of Boston, such as T. W. Higginson, Edward Everett Hale, and many others, were
merely transformed abolitionists themselves, increased
Howells' awareness of the need for re-examining his political views. Howells wrote to his father in November, 1890,
to console him for the loss of the local Republican ticket
in Ohio. His words carry the peculiar sincerity and confidence that always marked his relationship to his father;
they express, as nearly as Howells ever came to a definite
political declaration, his disgust with the old parties and his
hope for the new People's Party, then under discussion
among the Christian Socialists. Howells wrote:

You mustn't be too much cast down by the elections. I look
forward to the decay of both the old parties, and the growth of
a new one that will mean true equality and real freedom, and

not the images we have been mocked with hitherto. The poor Negroes whom we laughed at for expecting the government to give them each "forty acres and a mule," have a truer ideal of a civilized state than the manufacturers who want more and more tariff but won't raise their workman's wages a cent. Whatever we confess to the enemy, we must confess to ourselves, that in this matter the Republicans have been humbugging. . . . At the same time I have not the least faith in the Democrats. But my faith in the grand and absolute change, sooner or later, is so great that I don't grieve over their success. They are sure to abuse their victory, and then they will be out of power again, and I hope that a party "of the people, for the people" will rise up in their place, and make this a country where no man who will work need want.[9]

The party that Howells dreamt of in 1890 was the People's Party, which became the Populist Party of 1892, into which Bliss and many other members of the group were absorbed.

When Howells wrote the above letter, however, the tone of the meetings had not become exclusively political— though, indeed, many members of the Nationalist Club, organized by Edward Bellamy at this time, were also members of the Church of the Carpenter, a mission of the Episcopal Church, established by Bliss in Boston in 1890. Men and women of both groups were eagerly discussing ideas having to do with the regeneration of society in the light of early Christianity, unconfused by the creeds of churches. Tolstoy's *Que Faire?*, which Howells had recently reviewed, seems to have been studied by the whole group, each member of which might have said with Howells that Tolstoy gave him "heart to hope that the world may be made over in the image of Him who died for it." [10] Twenty years later, when Jane Addams recalled the opening of Hull House in Chicago in 1889, she compared her own feeling for the poor with those of Tolstoy expressed in *Que Faire?* She wrote:

Actual experience had left me in much the same state of mind I had been in after reading Tolstoy's "What to do," which is a description of his futile efforts to relieve the unspeakable distress and want in the Moscow winter of 1881, and his inevitable conviction that only he who literally shares his own shelter and food with the needy, can claim to have served them.[11]

Jane Addams, like most serious novel readers of the day, realized that Howells' determined fight for "realism," as opposed to "romance," was not merely a literary argument but was related to the growing awareness of the claims of a realistic approach to the problems of society. In *Twenty Years at Hull House*, she remarked:

Mr. Howells has said that we are all so besotted with our novel reading that we have lost the power of seeing certain aspects of life with any sense of reality because we are continually looking for the possible romance.[12]

A hitherto unpublished letter written by Howells at this time in behalf of an unemployed worker, suggests how seriously he was attempting to see the "reality" of the social problems in Boston without any "romance." The letter, addressed to a possible employer, reads: [13]

Boston, Feb. 21, 1890.

Gentlemen:

I visited to day for the Associated Charities a man named Adam Kaylan, employed till Christmas last at the Standard Sugar Refinery. He has had no work since, and has a wife and three children.

I venture to ask if you could find work for him. He tells me that he was employed in making bags.

Will you kindly send me a word of reply?

Yours Truly,

W. D. Howells.

The evolution of Howells' social beliefs towards a deeper sense of their underlying significance has been traced through *The Minister's Charge* (1887), *Annie Kilburn* (1889), and *A Hazard of New Fortunes* (1890), but their impact on Howells' generation has not been sufficiently studied. These novels were read and discussed in their own time, not merely for their literary interest but as contributions to an active social program. Howells' "Study" in *Harper's* of December, 1890, was a reflection of his Christian Socialist beliefs, simply stated, which grew out of the thought of this Boston world; it was addressed, however, to his wide circle of *Harper's* readers.[14] In this Christmas essay, Howells wrote that he wiped the dust and frost from the window of the "Editor's Study," and observed that a change had passed over the world, "tacit, but no less millenial," which was, alas, only a temporary warming of the heart caused once a year by "the Christmas spirit." During one month every year a certain sense of "brotherhood" prevailed when "it was plainly obvious that the old order was succeeded by the new; that the former imperfect republic of the United States of America had given place to the ideal commonwealth, the Synthetized Sympathies of Altruria"; this was, in turn, a province in the Federation of the World, "represented by a delegation eager to sacrifice their selfish interests in the Parliament of Man." The "Study" of December, 1890, gave the readers of *Harper's* their first glimpse of Altruria,[15] but the message was couched in such elaborate language that Howells' words could hardly have been interpreted by his readers as a plea for Christian Socialism.

However, by November, 1891, W. D. P. Bliss, editor of *The Dawn*,[16] "a journal of revolution toward practical Christianity," and the official organ of the Christian Socialists, was calling for stronger action, especially on the part of writers, preachers, newspaper men, and educators. Howells' *Annie Kilburn* was frequently listed in *The Dawn's* columns, perhaps as an example of "stronger action." As a more specific guide to action, Bliss stated the purpose of Christian Socialism in every issue of the magazine, to indicate the line of thought to be stressed. The movement existed, he said, to point out the need for church reform, to support the theory of labor unions, and to encourage reliance on the ballot rather than on revolution as a means of redressing social wrongs. Before Bliss resigned from his editorship, he wrote:

> Workingmen are learning fast that American justice and American laws exist mainly to keep workingmen down and protect property, while capitalists can disobey the laws *ad infinitum*. It is well. Workingmen must learn that they can gain nothing by appeal either to violence or legal proceeding. Their only way is to strike through the ballot and overcome the capitalistic ownership of property.[17]

During the seven years of his editorship, Bliss had urged all men and women who could write, speak, or teach, to lend support to these ideas by whatever means they could command. "The practical thing to do today is to educate. . . . We are sowing seed." [18]

Not only had Bliss advocated a pragmatic political approach, but he also had proposed the establishment on a farm outside of Boston of a Christian Socialist community, which he described in a two-column article.[19] Bliss and his followers dreamed of a loosely organized community that would, by laboring a few hours a day, solve the problem of poverty and wealth. He specifically denied any relationship between such an undertaking and that of Brook Farm, which, a generation earlier, had proved unsuccessful. No

initial investment was to be demanded nor were the partici-
pants expected to give up their ordinary means of liveli-
hood outside the community. They would merely share a
belief in Christianity and Brotherhood expressed in practical terms.

It will at least furnish a healthy home, where, making their
own lives full and right and true, in communion with the rest-
ful processes of nature, workers may gain rest and uplift and
inspiration to go out into the world and battle for the truer
vision.[20]

By literally following the teaching of Christ and his inter-
preters, from St. Paul to Tolstoy, Bliss believed that men
and women living on a farm together might illustrate the
concept of brotherhood as understood by the early Christians. Bliss's dream went no further than his proposal in *The
Dawn* of November, 1891; his demand for bolder social
and political action, however, was heard in widening circles, until, finally, it was absorbed into the platform of the
People's Party.

Howells' response to Bliss's appeal for practical aid was
a series of essays which soon began to appear, dealing with
a similar group of Christians, who were also in search of
"the truer vision." Though Howells had already made use
of many Christian concepts in *A Hazard of New Fortunes*,
in this new series of essays, called a "Romance," the reader
was carried one step further toward Christian Socialism;
he was, in fact, introduced to an actual community of
Christian Socialists expressing its belief in communal
living in a remote land called Altruria, rather than on a
farm outside of Boston. The attitude of the citizens toward
work and play, individual property, the use of the vote, as
well as the underlying sentiment of brotherhood, are all
akin to those found in every issue of *The Dawn*.

Bliss, indeed, had already described his dream of a church community in an article entitled, "Is it Coming?" which appeared in *The Dawn* of May, 1892—just six months before "A Traveller From Altruria" began in *The Cosmopolitan*. Bliss wrote:

Seven years ago the writer dreamed of a church different from any church he knew. It was to be a Brotherhood: its members were to live in little homes in an enclosure or close around the church. They were to meet in the church every morning for prayer and hymn. Then they were to work in some co-operative industry for the good of all. They were to meet for meals in a common banquet hall. There was to be a church school for the children. There was to be a co-operative laundry and other conveniences of life. In the evenings they were to meet in a churchhouse for dance and laughter, for music and instruction. There was to be a reading room and a library and reception room for all. The homes were to be simple and easily cared for, all by the women of the church in turns. Thus they would not be overworked with household cares but be true glad mothers of glad church children.[21]

"The dream," Bliss admitted, "has not yet all come true. We are in a city, though already a country house is being talked of." Undiscouraged, Bliss approached the problem of a co-operative community from another angle in the next issue of *The Dawn*.[22] His article for June, 1892, was headed "What Rich Men Can Do," and in it Bliss again let his imagination turn to his favorite dream. "But suppose," he wrote, "some rich, strong city church should turn itself into a co-operative community."

Bliss's hope for such a community might have been inspired by his friend and associate, the Reverend William S. Rainsford,[23] Rector of St. George's Protestant Episcopal Church on Stuyvesant Square, New York, who was mentioned by Bliss as one of the speakers at his Boston Mission.

Though the efforts of Dr. Rainsford and other clergymen to establish a Mission of the Church of the Carpenter in New York had failed, the Rector of St. George's had successfully worked to improve the social usefulness of his church. J. Pierpont Morgan,[24] a vestryman and later a warden of the Church, had made plain to all what rich men could do to extend the community usefulness of their churches. In 1888 Morgan had built a Parish House for St. George's that had become the model of such buildings all over the country, and two years later he established St. George's "Cottage-by-the-Sea" on Long Island to provide summer vacations for mothers and children of the New York poor. Howells, before he had moved to Boston in 1889, lived directly across the Park from St. George's, and it was to this Square that he returned when he took up his residence again in New York in 1892. Basil March, like Howells, whose alter ego he undoubtedly was, had the habit of wandering in and out of the churches in New York; later, in *Their Silver Wedding Journey*, Howells was to refer directly to St. George's, which, he said, he could see over the tops of the trees, from his living room window.[25] Here, then, was an example near at hand of the transforming power of practical Christianity.

Howells gave substance to Bliss's "dream" when, a few months after the appeal in *The Dawn*, he published the first chapter of "A Traveller From Altruria" in the newly revived *Cosmopolitan*. To many readers his "Romance" seemed mere fantasy; it was actually a reflection of the serious thought of the Christian Socialists of the 1890's.[26] That this hope of ameliorating the conditions of life for the masses was widely felt, and that Howells, in his Altrurian essays, was looked upon as a leader by the philanthropically inclined wealthy, as well as by the socialists with whom he had been associating, is evident. A description of a gathering of some of "the best minds among us," concerned with the question of how to plan "a better life" for the poor, may be found among the "Notes" made by Edmund Clarence Stedman, "shortly before his death" in 1908.[27] Stedman, himself a critic and poet—and Wall Street broker—was among the "very rich men" invited to "the beautiful town residence" of Whitelaw Reid, who had returned in 1892 from France, where he had been United States Minister. Though Stedman and Reid were old newspaper men whom Howells had known in his youth, both of them had now become wealthy and powerful. Henry Irving was the guest of honor at this luncheon for gentlemen, where "the company was select." Howells, however, was seated at the right hand of Reid and Stedman at his left, for Reid wished to indicate that literary men were appropriate associates for the wealthy, who were intent on using their fortunes for the improvement of social conditions. After seating his guests, "Mr. Reid then called upon the magnates present to drink the health of his friend Howells, a 'parlor anarchist,' and of myself, an 'amateur socialist.' " Apparently all glasses were lifted in honor of the two writers, for, as Stedman remembered the scene, "This pleasant vein of humor was merrily enough received and indeed I would accept my degree of *Am. Soc. Doc.* right willingly, since we were all amateurs . . . and amateurs confessedly care for what is rudimentary and emotional." The circle of guests looked with amusement at the small, smiling novelist in their midst with no realization of the depth of feeling behind his "amateur" effort to right the wrongs of society. Stedman, then more interested in his own business success than in socialism, also glanced somewhat patronizingly at his old friend, remarking in his notes that "the pleasantry of regarding

Mr. Howells, the sturdiest of men, as a parlor knight of any stripe, and Howells, the gospeller of peace and good-will, as an 'anarchist' with all that implies, was exquisite enough to travel far."

Howells' ideas on society, his "drastic arraignment of the way we live now," were, indeed, to travel further than those assembled at Whitelaw Reid's luncheon could have anticipated.

NOTES

1. *My Literary Passions* (1895), pp. 250–251.
2. *Life in Letters*, I, 404.
3. "Mr. Howells's Paper," *The House of Harper*, J. Henry Harper (1912), p. 322. For an account of a second letter regarding the Chicago Anarchists, which brought Howells again before the public, see John W. Ward, "Another Howells Anarchist Letter," *American Literature*, XXII (January, 1951), 489–490. See also Howells' comment, *Life in Letters*, I, 401.
4. Unpublished letter. Houghton Library, Harvard. Referred to by Budd, "Altruism Arrives in America," *op. cit.*, p. 40. Other unpublished letters from J. W. Harper, Jr., in the Houghton Library, indicate that Howells had talked over plans for a loosely compiled commentary on New York even before he joined the staff of *Harper's*. A letter of June 12, 1885, refers to "a *feuilleton* for 'Harper's Weekly,' embracing current social, literary & artistic topics, with story & incident,—which we could illustrate . . ." Harper would like to discuss this idea with Howells. In a letter of June 20, 1885, Harper said he hoped to have a Board Meeting, at which Howells' "fiction scheme" would be considered. On July 1, 1885, Harper asked Howells certain commercial questions concerning his proposed "Miscel-

lany of Fiction." Joseph Wesley Harper, Jr. was head of the firm in 1885. By the time Howells actually resigned from the "Study" in 1892, the position had been given to J. Henry Harper, a cousin of J. W. Harper. See *The House of Harper, op. cit.,* for a statement of the interrelations of this large family of editors and publishers. For Howells' own statement of his relation to the House, see especially Chapter XXV.

5. *Life in Letters,* I, 418–419.

6. "Editor's Study," *Harper's Monthly,* LXXVIII (December, 1888), 159.

7. *The House of Harper,* p. 323.

8. *Life in Letters,* II, 3.

9. *Ibid.,* pp. 8–9.

10. *My Literary Passions* (1895), p. 251.

11. *Twenty Years at Hull House* (1910), p. 260. Also see Howells' "Study," *Harper's* (December, 1888), *op. cit.*

12. *Idem.,* p. 307.

13. This letter is in the possession of the present writer.

14. "Howells and the Church of the Carpenter," Clara Marburg Kirk and Rudolf Kirk, *The New England Quarterly,* XXXII (June, 1959), 185–206.

15. "Editor's Study," *Harper's Monthly,* LXXXII (December, 1890), 152–156. After a brief opening, Howells turned to the real subject of the "Study," the Copyright Law. The terms, "Federation of the World" and "Parliament of Man," are borrowed from Tennyson's "Locksley Hall."

16. *The Dawn* was edited by W. D. P. Bliss from May, 1889, to March, 1896. Hamlin Garland, Francis Bellamy, Richard T. Ely, and others were assistant editors at various times during these years. In the December, 1890, issue of *The Dawn,* Bliss announced that he had purchased the publication from the Society of Christian Socialists, in order to make it more aggressive in its social program.

17. *The Dawn* (February, 1895), p. 2.

18. "What To Do Now," W. D. P. Bliss. *The Dawn* (July, 1890), p. 113.

19. The article is entitled "Proposed." *The Dawn* (November, 1891), pp. 7–8. In the same issue the following advertisement appeared: "To buy and carry on near Boston, a Union Farm, as the beginning of a Neighborhood or Fellowship of Christian Socialists. . . . Wanted: The right men and women to co-

operate in the enterprise." This issue of *The Dawn* was announced as "a People's Party issue." The Platform of the
People's Party was published in *The Dawn* of December, 1891.

20. "Proposed," *op. cit.*, p. 7.

21. P. 13.

22. P. 6.

23. Bliss recorded the fact that Dr. William S. Rainsford once
preached in the Church of the Carpenter. See "The Church of
the Carpenter and Thirty Years After," *The Social Preparation for the Kingdom of God*, Mid-Winter, 1922, IX (January,
1922), p. 15. See also "Christian Socialism in New York City,"
by R. Heber Newton, *The Dawn* (April, 1890), p. 1. On June
31, 1890, the Reverend R. H. Newton called a meeting in All
Souls' Lecture Room to organize a branch of the Society of
Christian Socialists in New York City, which was attended
by many clergymen. The movement was not successful.

24. Herbert L. Satterlee, *J. Pierpont Morgan: An Intimate Portrait*
(1939).

25. *Their Silver Wedding Journey* (1895), I, p. 21.

26. One of the undertakings which occupied Bellamy's attention
when he left the Boston group was the editing of the Nationalist's publication, *The New Nation*. As soon as "A Traveller From Altruria" began to appear in *The Cosmopolitan*, Bellamy welcomed it with a three-column article (November 26,
1892, p. 701) in which he recognized that this "very clever piece
of fantasy from Mr. Howells' pen" was a serious contribution
to the ideas on "our caste distinction based on wealth and
consequent occupation" and "give the lie to our pretension of
republican equality." Hardly had "A Traveller" been completed than Bellamy hailed it again as an important contribution to the widespread discussion of the evils of the competitive
system prevailing in America. "It is surely," he wrote, "a most
significant sign of the present trend of thought in this country,
and of the manner in which the hope of a near and radical
social transformation is taking hold of the best minds among
us, that the leading novelist of the times should have turned
aside from the conventional types of polite fiction to give his
countrymen this drastic arraignment of the way we live now,
and this glowing exposition of a nobler, higher, better life
which beckons us on." (October 14, 1893, p. 458.)

27. *The Life and Letters of Edmund Clarence Stedman* (2 vols.)

edited by Laura Stedman and George M. Gould (1910), II, 536–537. It is to be noted that Howells himself at this period of his life was to be numbered among the wealthy, though almost all that he earned annually came from his writing. According to Cady, Howells' yearly net income was $60,000 in 1890; $68,000 in 1892; $84,000 in 1894, and $93,000 in 1897. (Edwin H. Cady, *The Realist at War*, 1958, p. 192.) It was at the opening of this decade that Howells wrote to his father (February 2, 1890), after a visit with Mark Twain in Hartford, "He and his wife and Elinor and I are all of accord in our way of thinking: that is, we are theoretical socialists, and practical aristocrats." *Life in Letters*, II, 1.

Chapter II

The Cosmopolitan
New York, 1891–1892

An unexpected opportunity to enter the arena in response to Bliss's appeal was presented to Howells during the autumn of 1891; and, to the surprise of most of his friends, he seized it. In December, 1891, Howells resigned from *Harper's* to become coeditor of *The Cosmopolitan*, which had, in 1889, been purchased by John Brisben Walker, already well known both as a journalist and as a successful businessman.[1] The decision was reached suddenly, as Howells explained to Charles Eliot Norton, then in Cambridge. He wrote to Norton from "The Cosmopolitan Magazine, Editorial Department," December 12, 1891:

> Dear Friend,
>   I fancy that it must have been with something like a shock you learned of the last step I have taken, in becoming editor of this magazine. Nothing was further from my thoughts when I saw you a few weeks ago. The offer came unexpectedly about the beginning of this month, and in such a form that I could not well refuse it, when I had thought it over.[2]

Walker's offer, Howells explained, would free him from the necessity of placing his stories and bargaining about prices and would enable him thenceforth to complete a novel before beginning to print it.³ These were Howells' "selfish reasons for accepting the offer," and they were his first. His underlying reason—"the magazine is in such a state that I can hope to do something for humanity as well as the humanities with it"—was, however, the one that made him willing, after he had terminated his connection with the "Editor's Study," to turn to a fresh enterprise. Norton expressed his doubts about the undertaking in a prompt reply of December 19: "You will have a hard time to lift 'The Cosmopolitan' out of the atmosphere in which it has flourished,—an atmosphere in which there has been a large mingling of the vitreous oxide gas of second-rate vulgarity." Howells answered his Bostonian monitor on December 29: "What I shall be able to make of my new affair," he wrote, "I cannot promise. You know my ideals. I shall not lower them, and I cannot change them; for good or evil I cannot realize another's. That is my greatest safeguard; but the way seems open to do good, and I am hopeful." ⁴

Howells saw in Walker, who had himself been a visitor at the Church of the Carpenter, an editor with ideas that he thought might be akin to his own. Walker was, in fact, a recent convert to Catholicism, and shared the strong reforming zeal of this tradition, different but akin to that of the Episcopal Church, of which the Church of the Carpenter was a mission. Howells was full of enthusiasm for his new contact. "I am to be associated with the owner, Mr. John Brisben Walker," he wrote happily to Norton, "a man of generous ideal, who will leave me absolute control in literature, and whom I think with in many other matters."

The "many other matters," on which Howells assumed

that he and Walker agreed, stirred the curiosity, not only of Norton, but also of writers of literary columns of Boston and New York. That Howells, who had never showed an inclination to associate himself with fads and movements— who had, moreover, frequently declared his desire to give up all editing and to devote himself to his "fictioning"— should suddenly have decided to be coeditor of *The Cosmopolitan* with this wealthy, zealous newspaper man, exponent of the "new journalism," surely required a public explanation.

About ten days after his letter to Norton, Howells granted an interview in his New York home to a reporter of the *Boston Daily Advertiser*, who found Howells "pleasantly located in East Seventeenth Street." [5] The full-column article appeared on the editorial page of the December 26, 1891, issue of the *Advertiser*, under the heading, "Mr. Howells Talks. He Predicts much for The Cosmopolitan." Howells told his interviewer that his contract with *Harper's* would end with the appearance of his new novel, *The World of Chance*, and that then there would be an opportunity "to do something on the Cosmopolitan, and Mr. Walker and I intend to try to make it the best magazine in the world." [6]

Before the month was over, Hamlin Garland, one of the editors of *The Dawn*, also made a trip to New York and called on Howells in his new home. Garland, like the rest of the literary world, was eager to learn at first hand why Howells had agreed to a partnership with Walker. Garland's "chat" was printed in the *Boston Evening Transcript*, January 1, 1892, [7] in the same issue of which appeared an anonymous article on "Mr. Howells's Plans," announcing to the public that "unquestionably Mr. Howells will be a greater power than ever in the radical wing of American literature, and do his great work at less cost to himself." [8] Garland's report on Howells and his plans is in milder terms; he found Howells

living in a comfortable, old-style house on Seventeenth Street, which is in the very heart of this terrible city. It is a short walk from the magazine office, which is at the corner of Broadway and Twenty-fifth. . . . The talk of course drove very soon to the subject of his announced change of editorial chairs.

Howells gave Garland a factual account of Walker's flattering invitation to become coeditor of *The Cosmopolitan*. In Garland's words,

It had come to him as a complete surprise, changing many of his plans. Mr. Walker of The Cosmopolitan approached him on the matter by way of asking for a series of essays, but this seemed too much like the work he had been doing for *Harper's*, and which he felt he could no longer do profitably.

Having so recently resigned from the "Editor's Study" of *Harper's Monthly*,[9] Howells hesitated to undertake a regular editorial obligation, for he

was trying to escape from extra work of that character. He had felt for some time that the time had come when it could be given up. He felt that he had stated his position clearly, and that the continuation of such articles would necessarily be in the nature of reiteration.

Just as Fulkerson in *A Hazard of New Fortunes* was unwilling to accept Basil March's refusal to join the staff of *Every Other Week*, so Walker did not give up his hope of luring Howells to *The Cosmopolitan*. To quote Garland again:

Upon his refusal to do that specific work, Mr. Walker asked Mr. Howells to become an editor upon the magazine. This proposition appealed to Howells in a different way. It did not involve, apparently, any extra writing, but, on the contrary, offered a complete change of work.

Howells told Garland that he gave Walker's "generous proposition careful study," and at last accepted it.

Candid though Howells appeared to be in his talk with his Boston friend, a certain "flavor of an enigma" lingered about Howells' decision to link his fortunes to those of the rising editor of *The Cosmopolitan*. In his "Boston Letter" to the New York *Critic* the following week, Charles E. L. Wingate discussed the puzzle for the benefit of his readers: [10]

I am told that the foundation cause of Mr. Howells's assuming the editorship of *The Cosmopolitan* lay in a little white-covered pamphlet which appeared some two months ago. There is the flavor of an enigma in this, I admit, but perhaps when the name of the author of that pamphlet is mentioned an inkling will be given. It was John Brisben Walker.

Wingate was, no doubt, correct in assuming that his readers were familiar with the name of the new editor-owner of *The Cosmopolitan* who had rescued that publication from bankruptcy in 1889 and was now making it a rival of *Harper's, Scribner's,* and *Century*.[11] The "little white pamphlet," however, was certainly unknown to most of his readers. Wingate's description of it reminds one at once that Walker's journalistic instinct had prompted him to seek out the new ideas of the Christian Socialists that most appealed to Howells, and that these ideas he had incorporated into an address at the Catholic University, Washington.

The Critic's "Boston Letter" supplies us with the explanation of Howells' sudden decision to "do something for humanity" through *The Cosmopolitan*. Wingate here states:

Last March Mr. Walker delivered an address before the students of the Catholic University at Washington, and the effect of his bold words upon "The Church and Poverty" was so pronounced that he was led afterwards to put his address in print. I remember as I read the little book—and others will recall it now, if the words passed under their eye—how boldly Mr. Walker pointed out the danger to the nation that lay in poverty and in over-wealth as well; how candidly he called upon the clergy to look beyond becoming portly, well-fed, elegantly attired gentlemen, and, instead, to labor to reach the people. The waste in our economical system, Mr. Walker declared, was the cause of increasing the working hours one half. In no halting voice he called upon layman and priest to encourage the rich and protect the poor, to learn to produce wealth and to distribute it equitably. In these words, as I am told, Mr. Howells found so much that agreed with his own views that he immediately wrote Mr. Walker a letter of appreciation. The letter led to a meeting, the meeting to a discussion of business, the discussion to a proposal, and the proposal to the association of the two editors in *Cosmopolitan* work. Mr. Howells had already resigned from *Harper's*, so his leaving the old magazine was not the result of his connection with the new. An association begun with such a fraternal union in principles ought to be productive of emphatic results.[12]

A glance at Walker's speech of March 18, 1891, gives one a hint of the "fraternal union in principle" remarked upon by Wingate. For Walker, "well known as a thinker and a writer of great power," [13] did not hesitate to challenge the young postulants of the Catholic University, whom he was addressing in terms very like those used by the men and women associated with the Church of the Carpenter. "If you make of yourselves portly, comfortably fed, richly housed, elegantly attired gentlemen," he warned, "there will be something of justification in the doubt that you are the successors of Him who came in the guise of an humble carpenter's son." [14]

That the "fraternal union" of Howells and Walker had begun at least a year earlier is suggested by the Tables of Contents of *The Cosmopolitan* of 1890–1891. The editor himself had hailed Howells' *Hazard of New Fortunes* in a two-page article called "From the Editor's Window"; [15] Walker delighted in "the stream of humanity" that passed before the office window of *The Cosmopolitan*, at the corner of Broadway and Twenty-fifth Street, and he recognized in the crowd the characters that moved through Howells' novel. "One might almost fancy Mr. Howells himself a socialist," he mused as he contemplated Howells' presentation of the fiery, old Lindau. No, surely Mr. Howells was not precisely a socialist. But what "gives Howells his broad hold upon the American Public?" Walker asked. He answered his question by further queries:

Is it not his sympathy with human failings, even while holding them up to ridicule? Does he not try to teach? Has he not at heart the betterment of his fellows? Is he not sorry alike for the struggles of the poor for bread, and of the vulgar rich for social advancement? And if he is a socialist, why, then, the good God made us all socialists, of such a gentle, pitying, helpful kind, sorry for our brother's hunger and our own shortcomings.

Walker's comment on Howells' latest novel appeared in the March, 1890, issue of *The Cosmopolitan*, a few months after Walker's purchase of that magazine. One can well understand why Walker, in the autumn of 1891, approached Howells with the suggestion that together they might turn *The Cosmopolitan* into a magazine of first importance.

Before addressing himself to Howells, however, Walker again featured the novelist in his magazine. In November,

1890, an article entitled "Literary Boston," by Lilian Whiting, appeared in *The Cosmopolitan*, and here Howells was presented as the novelist speaking most emphatically to the readers of the present. The essay opened with a full description of Howells' career, his writing habits, and his home on Commonwealth Avenue. The paragraph ended with these words:

As a novelist, he may be said to be the prophet of the present; he is intensely modern; he is an earnest student of conditions and their tendencies; he is looking deeply into life on every side; nothing escapes him; nothing is trivial to him.[16]

Howells, for his part, must have found the Tables of Contents of *The Cosmopolitan* full of interest before he himself was connected with the magazine. Almost all of his specific social ideas later discussed by the Traveler—such as labor organizations, railroads, and their effect on impoverished New England farms, taxes and the function of money, the unregulated lumbering of our national forests, women as wage-earners and women in the home—were presented in the magazine when Walker was the sole editor. Howells' initial conversations with this crusading journalist who was tinged with Christian Socialism, were undoubtedly full of hopeful suggestion for the future of the country. Walker's articles, "A Modern City's Factors of Growth" (May, 1890) and "Alfalfa Farming at the Foot of the Rocky Mountains" (November, 1891), reflecting Walker's own recent experiences in building a fortune in Colorado, no doubt stirred Howells' interest in the social potentialities of the West. T. V. Powderly's long essay in the December, 1891, issue, "On Earth Peace, Good Will Towards Men," was a plea for trade unionism and the Knights of Labor in line with the ideas of Bellamy, Bliss,

Gronlund, and others with whom Howells was then associating in Boston.

Howells probably read with satisfaction, in the November, 1891, issue of *The Cosmopolitan*, Brander Matthews' three-page review of his own "Study" essays, gathered together the previous May in a small volume, *Criticism and Fiction*. This laudatory review was followed, in the next issue, by Matthews' comment on the new, illustrated edition of Howells' *Venetian Life*. Walker's practical success with *The Cosmopolitan*, impressive though that was, was perhaps less of a lure to Howells than the fact that the editor clearly was sympathetic with Howells' writing. In Walker, Howells thought, for a few months, that he had found the very partner with whom he might put into effect Bliss's plea for action on the part of writers.

Howells was further encouraged by the fact that Walker had already added to his staff other men well known for their enlightened views, who were also Howells' warm personal friends of long standing. The "Literary Notes" of the *Boston Evening Transcript*, January 2, 1892, lists these writers chosen by Walker to raise the level of *The Cosmopolitan* in all fields, social, political, and, finally, literary:

The announcement that Mr. Howells will leave Harper's Magazine, to take editorial charge of the Cosmopolitan, on March 1, calls attention to the process of building up the staff of a great magazine. The first step, after its editorial control was assumed by Mr. John Brisben Walker, was to add to it Edward Everett Hale, who took charge of a department called "Social Problems," subjects concerning which the greatest number of people are thinking today. Some months later a department was established called "The Review of Current Events." To take charge of this a man was needed who should be familiar not only with the great events of the past thirty years, but who knew personally the leading men both of the

United States and Europe who could interpret motives and policies. Murat Halstead accepted this position with the distinct understanding that his monthly review should be philosophical and never partisan. The next step in the history of the Cosmopolitan, was the placing of the review of the intellectual movement of the month in the hands of Mr. Brander Matthews, who for some time has been recognized as one of the two or three ablest critics in the United States. Finally came the acceptance of the editorship conjointly with Mr. Walker, by Mr. William Dean Howells. Mr. Howells, who is recognized universally as the foremost American novelist, upon the expiration of his contract with Harper Brothers, on the first of March will take in hand the destinies of a magazine which promises to exercise a share of influence with the reading classes of the United States. His entire services will be given to the Cosmopolitan, and everything he writes will appear in that magazine during the continuance of his editorship.

A perusal of *The Cosmopolitan* of November and December, 1891, suggests both why Howells thought he might "do something for humanity" by accepting Walker's invitation to join in the enterprise, and also why Walker wished to engage "the foremost American novelist" for his staff. Routine articles on life in remote lands, novelettes by little-known writers, instructions in needlework, biographies of historical characters—these were only partially redeemed by Edward Everett Hale's "Social Problems," Murat Halstead's "Review of Current Events," Brander Matthews' "Recent Essays in Criticism." The titles of these departments were not in themselves arresting perhaps, but the articles were written by men in the public eye.

Hale was recognized not only as the popular minister of the South Congregational Church in Boston, but also as a Christian Socialist interested in many causes. Halstead was a journalist from Ohio, much in the news for his liberal views. His nomination as minister to Germany two years earlier had been turned down by Congress because of a series of articles he had written on the sale of seats in Congress. Matthews, novelist and critic, had become known as a lecturer and, in 1892, was appointed Professor of Literature at Columbia University. Besides being specialists in three different fields, these men shared a social outlook that Howells had already expressed in his novels. For the first time the slogan, "From every man according to his ability; to everyone according to his needs," appeared in italics on the masthead of the January, 1892, issue of *The Cosmopolitan*. The motto reflected the views of Walker's outstanding new staff; it certainly gave Howells the "hope for humanity" that inspired him to turn his energies toward the undertaking.[17]

The announcement in the *Boston Evening Transcript* that the editor-owner of *The Cosmopolitan* had captured the man who had recently resigned from the staff of *Harper's* was followed in the February issue of *The Cosmopolitan* by Walker's brief notice, printed below a photograph of Howells by G. C. Cox which was used as a frontispiece of that issue. "On March the first," the sentence ran, "Mr. Howells will take editorial control of the Cosmopolitan Magazine conjointly with the present editor." In the same issue appeared a two-page article, "Mr. Howells and His Work" by Hjalmar Hjorth Boyesen. Here Howells' old friend observed that "a distinct growth, a broadening sympathy, has been perceptible in each new book which bears Mr. Howells' name," and, further, that "he has the courage of his convictions, and can fight for them right valiantly when occasion demands."[18]

So insatiable was the public curiosity concerning How-

ells' move from Boston to New York that over a page of
Frank Leslie's Weekly (March 17, 1892), signed by the
interviewer, Franklin Smith, was devoted to "An Hour
With Mr. Howells." The article begins with this fine flour-
ish: "Boston has finally lost Mr. W. D. Howells forever.
Hereafter, until the end of the story, New York can boast
of the honor so long enjoyed by the sister city." [19]

Howells' new home on Stuyvesant Square, the view
from his library window, his thoughts on the advantages
of Boston, New York, Paris, and London as literary cen-
ters, the importance of criticism to a novelist—all these
topics and many more were explored by the reporter
seated in Howells' comfortable study. Smith no doubt cor-
rectly judged the appetites of his readers for details about
their favorite novelist when he also reported that on the
table of the library "is a little silver ink-stand resting on
a piece of blotter," and not far away a silver knife, a pen
and a pencil, as well as a "little lexicon."

The interview in *Leslie's Weekly* was timed to Walker's
announcement in the February issue of *The Cosmopolitan*
that the new editor would assume his role in March. Howells' influence, however, was not apparent until the May
issue of the Magazine, and this, curiously enough, is the
only number that can be said to bear the unmistakable
stamp of Howells. In this issue, which opened with a handsome photograph of James Russell Lowell facing an elabo-
rately illustrated poem by the poet, we find the responses
to Howells' appeals to his friends for support in the new
venture.[20] Hamlin Garland, Henry James, T. W. Higginson, Sarah Orne Jewett, Clarence Stedman, Frank Stockton, and E. E. Hale, all mailed in their essays, stories, and
poems.[21] The "literary" tone of the issue was further en-

hanced by a play from Howells himself—"Evening Dress." Though the names of James, Lowell, and Pyle are found in the Tables of Contents of the June and July issues of *The Cosmopolitan*, no such bill-of-fare as that of May, 1892, ever graced subsequent issues.

On June 30 we find Howells writing to his father,

> I may as well tell you now that I have broken with my fellow editor, and shall cease to be connected 'officially' with *The Cosmopolitan* after to-day, though I may arrange to write regularly for it. My name will come off the title page after August. It was a great mistake ever to let it go on, but I feel great relief in the result. Some time I will tell you all the why and wherefore; but in large it was hopeless incompatibility.[22]

Howells had laid his plans with Walker in Boston, during the autumn and winter of 1891; he had aspired to make this rapidly rising magazine "the best in the world," and he had lost no time in writing to his faithful friends for aid. After this initial enthusiasm, however, Howells' interest flagged, nor did he ever fully explain why the new venture suddenly seemed no longer feasible. Perhaps his confidence was somewhat shaken by the attitude of his friends, for in spite of their generous responses, more than one contributor expressed surprise at the new turn in Howells' career. "But what is the Cosmopolitan?" Henry James asked in a letter in which he promised a contribution. James frankly declared that he believed Howells was being false to his genius as a writer of American chronicles in burdening himself with the care of editorship; Norton, after expressing his regret that he had already mailed to *Scribner's* a recent poem by Lowell, wrote that he was interested in Howells undertaking the editorship of *The Cosmopolitan*, since he would no doubt have an opportunity to raise the magazine out of its atmosphere of vulgarity. An unpublished note from Walker to Howells hinted that Howells had already voiced some of his own misgivings to his coeditor. Walker assured Howells that he had no cause for fears about the future of *The Cosmopolitan;* he was certain, he said, that his and Howells' judgment would "coincide most of the time." The staff of *The Cosmopolitan* would avoid troubling him, Walker wrote. Though "powerful interests" were undoubtedly against them both, he and Howells were bound to go forward, because both of them were now "before the public." [23]

Despite these reassurances, we know Howells had faced the New York undertaking with hesitation. The two years in Boston, then drawing to a close, had given him a firmer grasp of his own thinking by bringing him in contact with a group of men and women imbued with an aggressive Christian approach to social problems, which he thought was shared by the editor-owner of *The Cosmopolitan.* Though the move to New York had put Howells more "in the current of events," as he had wished to be, the daily pressures and annoyances of coediting a magazine with Walker had seemed to increase.[24] The irritation, apparently, was felt only by Howells, for Walker remained delighted by the name as well as the personality of his coeditor. As Howells wrote his father, "The best thing about [the arrangement] is Mr. Walker's infatuation with his bargain; yet it is terrible, in a way, to have a man so satisfied with you." [25]

Not only did Howells find his new working conditions intolerable [26] but he found himself, in the autumn of 1891, oppressed by the very thought of returning to the great metropolis. He confessed to his father, in a letter of October 18, that he "looked forward to a winter in New York with loathing." The daily sight of poverty and squalor in New York depressed Howells on his return to the city, as it had when he first encountered it. On March 20, 1892, Howells wrote to Norton, "I lay yesterday wondering at the great mass of human suffering and getting a kind of objective perception of its bulk and variety. What a hideous spectacle life is from that point of view." [27] Though Walker, too, was aware of "the great mass of human suffering" in the world around him, and abounded in schemes for alleviating it, he and Howells were not able to continue for more than a few months their plans for making *The Cosmopolitan* "the best magazine in the world."

Howells apparently took pains to conceal his disappointment, however. Only one week before writing this letter to his father, he allowed a three-column interview entitled "Mr. Howells, His Career, His Present Work and His Literary Opinions" to appear in the Sunday edition of the *New York Daily Tribune*.[28] The article was signed by T. C. Crawford, and included the following untroubled paragraph:

When at his new post as joint editor of "The Cosmopolitan Magazine" he occupies a small den in the Madison Square Bank Building, where there is room for a huge desk, a stuffed leather chair for Mr. Howells, and for three or four chairs for the literary aspirants who come trembling to submit to his judgment the samples of spring poetry, essays and stories which come in endless procession.

A few days after the appearance of this interview, Howells quietly left "the small den," perhaps to the surprise of the trembling literary aspirants. So unobtrusive was Howells' withdrawal, indeed, that the "dissolution" of this "literary compact" was not remarked upon by the *Brooklyn Daily Eagle* until the following autumn. The September 16, 1892, issue carried an editorial, "Mr. Howells, Novelist and Editor," in which the unidentified writer congratulated the novelist on his withdrawal from the role of editor, without in any way having made the resignation a personal issue.[29]

Though Howells gave up the coeditorship of *The Cosmopolitan* as suddenly as he had assumed it, he by no means severed his relationship with Walker, even though Howells found him "so much a man of mood." These editors were unable to work together in the office of the magazine on which they collaborated for a few brief months. They shared similar hopes and fears, however, as they viewed the social scene of the early 1890's. At the very time, for example, when Howells and Walker were terminating their uneasy editorial connection, a steel strike in Homestead, Pennsylvania, was attracting the attention of both men. In the course of the next few months they expressed, independently, similar views of the underlying question of labor in a democracy. An unpublished letter of July 14, 1892, from Walker to Howells [30] indicates that their common interest in social ideas was sufficiently strong to sustain them after the collapse of their joint efforts on *The Cosmopolitan*. In this letter Walker told Howells of the essay he planned to write for the September issue, "The 'Homestead' Object Lesson," and expressed his delight with the name Howells had proposed for his essays, "A Traveller From Altruria." Walker wrote that he was very hopeful of results from Howells' brain, once it set itself "to work upon the problems which concern humanity." This serial, which began two months later in the same magazine, reflected at a further distance Howells' views on "the Homestead affair," as well as his ideas on other current questions.

NOTES

1. John Brisben Walker (1847–1931) was born near Pittsburgh. His varied career began with two years at West Point, from which he resigned in 1868, in order to go to China with the new minister to Peking. On his return two years later he became an iron manufacturer in West Virginia. After making and losing a fortune, he wrote a series of articles on the mineral industry for Murat Halstead's *Cincinnati Commercial-Gazette*, that led to an appointment as managing editor of the *Pittsburgh Telegraph* in 1876 and thence to a position on the *Washington Chronicle*. When that paper was discontinued, Walker bought a 1600-acre ranch near Denver on which he raised alfalfa. He sold this property at a large profit in 1889, came to New York and bought the struggling *Cosmopolitan*, which he edited until he sold the magazine to William Randolph Hearst in 1905. In the first five years of his editorship, Walker raised the circulation from 16,000 to 400,000 and reduced the price to 10 cents a copy. For an account of Walker's early career, see "The Napoleon of the Magazines," *The New York Herald*, September 3, 1893, p. 13. For accounts of his later career, see obituaries in the *New York Times*, July 8, 1931, p. 8, and the *New York Herald*, July 8, 1931, p. 19. See also D. N. Rein, "Howells and The Cosmopolitan," *American Literature*, 17 (March, 1949), 49–50.
2. *Life in Letters*, II, 19.
3. Walker "secured Mr. Howells as editor of his magazine at a salary of virtually $15,000 a year." Stated in "The Napoleon of the Magazines," *op. cit.*
4. Unpublished letter. Houghton Library, Harvard.

5. 241 East Seventeenth Street, New York City.
6. P. 3. The article is half a column in length and contains a report of Howells' views on fiction and realism as already expressed in the "Study" of *Harper's Monthly*. The column was signed by the name of Spencer H. Coon, and was dated, "New York, Dec. 24." The *Boston Daily Advertiser* of January 2, 1892, p. 4, carried a brief announcement of the change in the editorship of *Harper's* "Study." The *Boston Daily Advertiser* was edited until 1868 by Charles Hale, brother of Edward Everett Hale. At the time of the interview with Howells, the paper was edited by William Emerson Barrett.
7. The Garland interview was reprinted in *The Critic*, January 9, 1892, p. 28.
8. The unidentified writer of the article commented, "The announcement that Mr. Howells had decided to give up 'The Study' in Harper's and that he had accepted an editorial position with the Cosmopolitan is a significant literary event. Mr. Howells has come to stand for the most vital and progressive principle in American literature and to have him assume editorial charge of a magazine means a great deal to the conservative as well as to the more radical wing of our literary public."
9. Though he had resigned several months earlier, Howells' last "Editor's Study" appeared in the March, 1892, issue of *Harper's*. On November 18, 1891, Walker wrote to Howells asking him to write a series of essays for *The Cosmopolitan*. Unpublished letter. Houghton Library, Harvard.
10. January 12, 1892.
11. The turning point in the fortunes of *The Cosmopolitan* came in November, 1892; "thereafter it was a profitable magazine." Frank Luther Mott, *History of American Magazines* (1957), p. 484. See "The Making of an Illustrated Magazine," *The Cosmopolitan*, XIV (January, 1893), 259–271. One hundred thousand copies of this issue were sold.
12. *The Critic*, XVII (January 16, 1892), 41. Quoted in part by Rein, *op. cit.*
13. The *Washington Evening Star*, March 19, 1891. The occasion was reported by the *Star* as follows: "The lecture room of the Catholic University was filled yesterday afternoon with an intelligent audience that listened with close attention to a lecture by John Brisben Walker, Ph.D. Mr. Walker is well known as a thinker and writer of great power, and his lecture

was in some respects a remarkable effort in the boldness with which he brought home to clergy and laymen their responsibility for many of the social difficulties that beset our civilization. No such plain speaking has been heard upon a platform under similar circumstances, and for this reason, as well as because of the food for thought to every one interested in the welfare and prosperity of his race and the government under which we live, an extended report of the lecture is given."

14. *The Church and Poverty* (no date), pp. 6–7.
15. *The Cosmopolitan,* VIII (March, 1890), 638–640.
16. *Idem.,* X (November, 1890), 207.
17. Walker wrote to Howells from St. Augustine, Florida, on February 23, 1892. In this letter Walker commented on Howells' charming farewell to the "Editor's Study" in the March, 1892, *Harper's*. Walker then remarked on the poverty in the South, which, he said, made him contemptuous of himself for the luxury in which he lived. Unpublished letter. Houghton Library, Harvard.
18. Pp. 502–503.
19. Vol. LXXIV, 118–119. Walker clipped this article and mailed it to Howells. Unpublished letter. Houghton Library, Harvard. The letter is dated by another hand, "Feb. (?) 1892." It was probably written in March, after the article had appeared.
20. Unpublished letters. Houghton Library, Harvard.
21. In the May, 1892, issue of *The Cosmopolitan* appeared "At the Brewery," by Hamlin Garland; "Wolcott Balestier," by Henry James; "School, College and Library," by T. W. Higginson; "The Passing of Sister Barsett," by Sarah Orne Jewett; "Falstaff's Song," by Clarence Stedman; "Asaph," by Frank Stockton; "Where Shall Polly Go To School?" by Edward Everett Hale. Other contributors among Howells' friends and acquaintances to the May, June, and July issues of the magazine were T. S. Perry, J. B. Harrison, M. Halstead, Brander Matthews, Theodore Roosevelt, H. H. Boyesen, and John Hay.
22. *Life in Letters,* II, 24.
23. Unpublished letter. Houghton Library, Harvard.
24. *Life in Letters,* II, 18.
25. *Life in Letters,* II, 20.
26. *Idem.,* p. 24. Frank Luther Mott quotes an assistant editor of *The Cosmopolitan* as saying that Mr. Walker "was a czar in his own world." The same editor, says Mott, tells "a legend

to the effect that once, when Howells was editor of the Cosmopolitan, he found a note upon his desk one morning, requesting that he report for duty at the unconscionable hour of eight o'clock. Yes, even Mr. Howells!" Mott, *op. cit.*, p. 483.

27. Unpublished letter. Houghton Library, Harvard.
28. June 26, 1892, p. 14.
29. P. 18.
30. Houghton Library, Harvard.

Chapter III

The Traveler
in New Hampshire
Summer, 1892

Soon after Howells left New York for the summer at the end of June, 1892, news of the strike at the Carnegie Iron and Steel Company's factory at Homestead, Pennsylvania, filled the papers. Not only did the employers fail to recognize the Amalgamated Association of Steel and Iron Workers, but they declared that unless their employees returned to work by July 1, willing to accept reduced wages, their places would be filled by nonunion men. The workers refused to accept these terms, and were met on the designated day by the gunfire of Pinkerton men, imported by the Company in armored barges. In the course of the battle, which raged from dawn until evening, nine detectives and eleven workmen were killed. The remaining Pinkerton men were, it is said, treated brutally after their surrender by the mob, even as they were being taken into hospitals.

Howells' conflicting feelings about these facts, which he read day after day in the newspapers,[1] are reflected in a letter to his father written from Intervale, New Hampshire, on July 10, 1892. Behind Howells' words one hears overtones of the thought of the Christian Socialists, who, though sympathetic with the workers, were against violence and in favor of mediation. "I suppose you have been as excited, as I have been, by the Homestead affair," Howells wrote. Sympathizing with the workers, he continued, "It is hard to remember that the men are playing a lawless part." Strikes "are no remedy"; they are only a reminder that "the trouble must go on as long as competition goes on." Howells' conclusion reflected the teaching of the early church, which the Church of the Carpenter sought to imitate:

> I come back to my old conviction, that every drop of blood shed for a good cause helps to make a bad cause. How much better if the Homesteaders could have suffered the Pinkertons to shoot them down unarmed. Then they would have had the power of martyrs in the world.[2]

Martyrdom, rather than bloodshed, was, of course, the choice of the early Christians, on whom the Christian Socialists based their beliefs. Howells believed that no social evolution based on genuine justice could be brought about without a Christian concept of brotherhood behind it.[3] These same ideas had recently been expressed by W. D. P. Bliss in the June, 1892, issue of *The Dawn*, in an article entitled, "What is Christian Socialism?" "Socialists do not of necessity believe in revolution . . . most are evolutionist," he had observed before the fatal events in Homestead. "They know that it must come slowly, if it comes to endure," Bliss had written. Finally, socialism is not the carrying out of any particular scheme: "The central principle is that more and more capital should be turned from competing ownership into public ownership." This article and others like it supplied Howells with the basic ideas with which he read the events of the summer.

Before the month was over, the workers had worsened their position in the eyes of those who believed in evolution rather than revolution. On July 24 Howells read in his newspaper that Henry C. Frick, President of the Carnegie Iron and Steel Company, had been shot twice and stabbed the previous day in his office by a compositor on a New York paper. In his next letter to his father,[4] Howells lamented this "wicked and foolish mistake," which only "makes a blood mist through which the situation shows wrong." And in one thing the labor side was surely wrong, Howells wrote. "It has the majority of votes, and can *vote* the law it wants, and it won't, but prefers to break the laws we share. This must come to an end, and probably will soon." Howells' belief in the efficacy of the vote and his confidence that progress in labor disputes could be made by democratic methods were shared by John Brisben Walker, who was also reflecting upon the daily dispatches from Homestead.

Walker's interpretation of "the Homestead affair" was clearly expressed in similar terms in his essay, "The Homestead Object Lesson," which appeared in the September, 1892, issue of *The Cosmopolitan*.[5] "The fact is," he said, "we have two separate worlds in this country," that of the rich and that of the poor. We have, however, the vote, and this gives us the hope that "the tendency to thought among the rich and the advance of intelligence among the poor" might bring about a solution. "Thank God, [the workers] are men who love the Republic and who hope for the elevation of their people through the evolution of the law. Certainly arbitration would seem a more modern method of interference than bayonets."

While Walker was preparing his article for the September issue of his magazine and Howells was imagining the views of his Altrurian, Bliss was throwing all of his weight toward the People's Party. "Homestead has sent thousands upon thousands of brave workingmen and men of thought of all classes into the People's Party," he wrote in an editorial commenting on the eventful summer for *The Dawn* of October, 1892.[6] "Now is America's time of trial," he pointed out, expressing the feeling of both Walker and Howells and many other "men of thought" of that decade.

"What Christian Socialists Believe Should Be Done Now" was the title of an article by Bliss in this same issue of *The Dawn*. "In order to be rich to-day," he said in terms not unlike those Howells put into the mouth of Basil March, "one must forget the golden rule, and push and plot and combine for self." Those who are capable of thought should read, write, and study the issues for "one ounce of justice is worth ten pounds of charity."[7] Only through the ballot box can Christian Socialism find expression; therefore, "let all the people legislate, by popular voting, on all important measures." These were the ideas on which Bliss had been hammering during the two years Howells spent in Boston; they were soon to reappear in the mouth of Mr. Homos, who discussed with his American friends the concept of trade unions in a society based on Christian ethics.[8]

In *A Traveler From Altruria* it was neither the minister nor the novelist but the banker who discussed with Mr. Homos the use of violence by both capital and labor during strikes. Such methods can be avoided, said the banker, only when the worker learns the power of the vote. Perhaps, ventured Mr. Twelvemough, the "un-American Socialists" stir up the strikes. "Why, no," returned Mr. Bullion, with calm authority, "I shouldn't say that." He then continued:

As far as I understand it, the socialists are the only fellows among them who propose to vote their ideas into laws, and nothing can be more American than that. . . . I'm not talking of anarchists, mind you, but of socialists, whose philosophy is more law, not less, and who look forward to an order that cannot be disturbed.

"But might not a rigid industrial system controlled by law mean a new sort of enslavement?" someone in the group suggested. "The new slavery would not be like the old," mused the banker. "The proletariat would probably be owned by the state, as it was at one time in Greece," he added. Moreover, there would be less suffering now than in pagan days, for "we have not had nineteen hundred years of Christianity for nothing." At this point the banker paused, and, to the relief of Mr. Twelvemough, broke into a laugh, and laid his hand upon the shoulder of Mr. Homos. "You see," he said, "I'm a kind of Altrurian myself. What is the reason why we should not found a new Altruria here on the lines I've drawn?" No reason at all, replied Mr. Homos; the people of Altruria, too, on the basis of the experience of Greece, modified by Christianity, debated the question as to "whether capital should not own labor, instead of labor owning capital." He added, ironically, "That was several hundred years ago," [9] before the whole idea of competition was outgrown.

Howells and Walker were united in their efforts to bring up to date the social thinking of the country. They both believed in the solution of social problems by means of the vote, aided by labor arbitration and unionism; and both of them reflected the views of Christian Socialism toward competitive capitalism. Though they found it difficult to work together, the sympathies of Howells and Walker were sufficient to permit Howells to continue his relationship with *The Cosmopolitan* as a contributor though not as a coeditor. "The Lounger" in *The Critic* of September 24, 1892, reported on the new arrangement in the following paragraph:

Mr. W. D. Howells will begin in the November *Cosmopolitan* a department attractively entitled "A Traveler From Altruria." . . . As no man can successfully edit a magazine and write its leading department as well, Mr. Howells has been relieved of all editorial work by Mr. Walker, the proprietor of the monthly, who has really been its editor ever since the property passed into his hands. I am very glad to hear of this change, for, while Mr. Howells might have succeeded very well as an editor, I enjoy him more as a writer. When he conducted the Editor's Study in *Harper's Monthly*, his caustic criticisms kept the teeth of two continents on edge. He broke the images before which we had prostrated ourselves for a lifetime, and caused our hair to stand on end with astonishment. . . . He gave us an intellectual shock that was not without its stimulating effect. Now he will open fire through the pages of *The Cosmopolitan*, and his shot, like that of the embattled Concord farmers, will be "heard round the world."

Howells "opened fire" the following month. The November, 1892, issue of *The Cosmopolitan* appeared with the title in bold red type across the cover of the magazine. In the first of Howells' twelve essays reflecting the Traveler's views, the author coped with the problems raised by "two separate worlds" in our American society, that of the rich and that of the poor. These essays, discussed with Walker before Howells left New York, were composed for the most part during a summer in "the beautiful pine woods" of Intervale, near North Conway, New Hampshire. Neither "the wind, or sun, or balsam" [10] of this retreat could counteract the impact of the newspaper accounts of the "Homestead affair"; Howells found relief in turning to his essays defining an Altrurian America where fierce competitiveness might be superseded by Christian Socialism. Whether "his shot" was "heard round the world" is a question; it was certainly heard by his generation as important comment on more than one of the issues of the day. Just as Howells had used his essays from the "Editor's Study" in the 1880's to shock his readers into an appreciation of the new "realism" in literature, so he now used his monthly essays in *The Cosmopolitan* to urge a more realistic attitude toward social problems.

It was not the newspapers alone that disturbed Howells peace by reminding him of the real problems of the world. Intervale itself proved no pastoral retreat to him, for the daily sight of burnt-over stretches of virgin forest and impoverished farms carried a message to his already disturbed mind, which only augmented that of the steel strikes of Pennsylvania. The effect on the Altrurian of country squalor was noted at the very outset of the essays Howells was composing. In Chapter II Mr. Twelvemough brought his guest to "a naked knoll overlooking the lake" at which the Altrurian stared in "a kind of horror."

It was a squalid ruin, a graceless desolation, which not even the pitying twilight could soften. The stumps showed their hideous mutilation everywhere; the brush had been burned and the fires had scorched and blackened the lean soil of the hill slope, and blasted it with sterility.[11]

On this sterile land lived the destitute farmers with their sad-eyed wives and troops of children. As Howells described one of these wooden cottages on the border of the forest,

the bare, curtainless windows were set in the unpainted frames, but the front door seemed not to be hung yet. The people meant to winter there, however, for the sod was banked up against the wooden underpinning; a stove-pipe stuck out of the roof of a little wing behind. While I gazed, a young-looking woman came to the door, as if she had been drawn by our talk with the children, and then she jumped down from the threshold, which still wanted a doorstep, and came slowly out to us.[12]

These glimpses of "the problem of poverty," set in a green countryside in the pleasant summer of 1892, brought Howells back to the "terrible quandry" of the poor. The conversation between Mr. Twelvemough, Mrs. Makely (Mrs. On-the-Make?) and the Altrurian suggested the debate in Howells' own mind as to the solution offered by Christian Socialism. Turning to the Altrurian, Mr. Twelvemough began, "And now see what difficulties beset us in dealing with the problem of poverty."

"I see," the Altrurian answered, "It is a terrible quandry."
"I wish," said Mrs. Makely, "that you would tell us just how you manage with the poor in Altruria."
"We have none," replied the Traveler.
"But the comparatively poor—you have some people who are richer than others?"
"No. We should regard that as the worst incivism."
"What is incivism?"
Mr. Twelvemough interpreted, "Bad citizenship."
"Well then, if you will excuse me, Mr. Homos," she said, "I think that is simply impossible. There *must* be rich and there *must* be poor. There always have been, and there always will be. . . . Didn't Christ himself say 'The poor ye have always with you?' "

The Altrurian looked at Mrs. Makely with an amazement visibly heightened by the air of complacency she assumed after delivering this poser: "Do you really think Christ meant that you *ought* always to have the poor with you?" he asked.

"Why, of course!" she answered triumphantly. "How else are the sympathies of the rich to be cultivated? The poverty of some and the wealth of others, isn't that what forms the great tie of human brotherhood? If we were all comfortable, or all shared alike, there could not be anything like charity, and Paul said, 'The greatest of these is charity.' I believe it's 'love' in the new version, but it comes to the same thing."

"The Altrurian gave a kind of gasp and then lapsed into a silence." [13] No doubt Howells overheard just such sentiments expressed by summer visitors, rocking in their wicker chairs on the wide pavilion of his New Hampshire hotel.

The problem of the relationship between unchecked lumbering, burnt-over farms, and country squalor, however, had been present in Howells' imagination at least ten years before the conversations between Mrs. Makely and the Altrurian found their place in his essays. When Howells was editing the *Atlantic*, he reviewed a book entitled *Dangerous Tendencies in American Life*, by The Reverend J. B. Harrison, Secretary of the New Hampshire Forestry Commission,[14] in which Harrison put before the reader the warnings, not heeded until more than a generation later, in regard to the use of our national forests. Howells had for many years known personally the author of this book. A brief reference to Harrison in one of Howells' letters to his father suggests that their friendship had been resumed during the summer of 1892:

I have been hearing lately from my old friend, J. B. Harrison, who used to write such strong papers for the *Atlantic*. He came originally from Green Co., O., but he now lives in New Hampshire, where he is head of the State forestry commission. Of course he is a kind of socialist. I enclose some of his letters, which may interest you, and I will send you two of his little pamphlets.[15]

If Howells had not read the book Harrison wrote in 1889, in collaboration with the well-known landscape architect and conservationist, Frederick Law Olmsted,[16] he certainly was, as an editor, thoroughly acquainted with Harrison's article, "The State and the Forest," in *The Cosmopolitan* for July 1892. This issue must have reached Howells at the very time when he was strolling around the New England countryside, viewing with dismay the desolation in the midst of the rich summer verdure. The comments of Mr. Homos have a basis in Harrison's assertions that the White Mountain area was so lumbered and burnt over that many farms were already ruined. "The utter desolation of these tracts shows what is the destiny of a large proportion of the White Mountain region if nothing adequate is done to interfere," Harrison warned. "The ruin is not coming rapidly, but it is coming surely," he continued.

More and more of the whole region will be cut off and afterwards burned over, till in time there will be vast areas of the mountain country of northern New Hampshire in which there will be no timber or shade or verdure or springs of water.[17]

Howells' remark to his father that of course Harrison "is a kind of socialist" sprang from the firm belief, expressed by Harrison in this essay, that "we should have state forestry in New Hampshire on a very extensive scale." Instead of protecting its forest, however, the state had already sold vast areas to private owners in 1867, and, as Harrison lamented, New Hampshire did not now possess "a single forest acre."

Though Howells might have hoped to enjoy country pleasures after a difficult winter, the arrival of the morning paper and the magazine from which he had so recently resigned, as well as his walks across the surrounding farms, served to remind him of the drastic need for a deepening of our social thinking. The Altrurian essays Howells was at that time composing reflect the dichotomy in Howells' mind. His half-whimsical linking of the characters of Mr. Twelvemough and Mr. Homos, as bland host and inquiring guest, was a partial resolution of his own despair in the face of inequalities between factory owners and strikers, lumber owners and farmers, the interests of the railroads and those of the country dwellers.[18] Mr. Twelvemough was eager to lead Mr. Homos across the meadow toward the lake and into "the tender gloom of the forest," there to listen to the music of the hermit thrushes, but unpleasant aspects of our social problems insisted on asserting themselves. Mr. Homos, unfailingly polite as he was, often found himself lapsing into silence at the unchristian attitudes which lay behind the injustices and cruelties noticeable even on a summer holiday. Thus Mr. Twelvemough and Mr. Homos reflected the debate in Howells' own conscience after he had learned to look at his world through the eyes of a Christian Socialist. "There are moments," admitted Mr. Twelvemough, "when [the Altrurian] seems so entirely subjective with me that I feel he is no more definite or tangible than a bad conscience." [19]

Howells' "bad conscience" was resolved, at least for the moment, in the Altrurian essays which began to appear the following November in *The Cosmopolitan.* No doubt he was moved to look at the desolate farms near his comfortable hotel with more insight because of the fact that his two years in Boston, as well as his unsuccessful attempt to work with Walker the previous winter, had made him more aware of the increased seriousness of the social problems both in city and country. In the essays, which reflected his inner conflict, Howells unobtrusively moved from the complacency of Mr. Twelvemough and identified himself with the Altrurian. With his old friend Harrison, Howells turned into "a kind of socialist" as he viewed the plight of the people in the "Age of Accumulation."

Charles E. L. Wingate's "Boston Letter" for *The Critic* of January 14, 1893, included the following paragraph, in which a letter from Howells to Harrison was quoted:

I think *The Critic's* readers will be interested in the letter which William D. Howells has written to the Secretary of the Forestry Commission in New Hampshire. . . . The letter was the outcome of the novelist's sojourn at North Conway, I presume, for certainly even a few months among the trees of the White Mountains must stir any lover to an appeal for their preservation. "You and I love trees," writes Mr. Howells, "perhaps more than dollars, but if we were hill-country farmers and saw that a bit of woodland would help us to pay our heavy taxes and live a little longer in the old house, we would sell the trees and rejoice in the dollars. Let the dollars come from the State, and your people will keep both the trees and the dollars." So, for this reason, Mr. Howells is willing to help the Commission in the effort to have the state buy the woodlands of New Hampshire and hold them forever. He adds this vigorous opinion:—"We talk about public spirit as if it were something the individual could rightly be expected to cherish to his loss, but that is nonsense; the only public spirit possible or even desirable is that which the public has." [20]

The "intellectual shock" which "The Lounger" of *The Critic* hoped Howells would give his readers when his Altrurian essays should begin to appear in *The Cosmopolitan* was felt because Howells was here reflecting upon the well-known social problems of his day. The steel strikes of Pennsylvania and the misuse of our national forests were merely two examples of "the shots" clearly heard by his contemporaries when Howells "opened fire" in Walker's interesting magazine. The greatest shock, perhaps, lay in the fact that Howells, through Mr. Homos, pointed out the growing conflict between competitive capitalism and Christianity. "I do not see why the Altrurian system should be considered so very un-American," [21] the Traveller observed at last—unless, of course, capitalism and Christianity should prove irreconcilable in America.

Walker, upon the receipt of the manuscript for this installment of "A Traveller," wrote a note to accompany his monthly check in which he commented with admiration on the directness and vigor of Howells' Altrurian. He enclosed in the envelope newspaper clippings praising Howells' "magnificent work." [22] Later in the same month,[23] Walker mailed to Howells another batch of clippings, this time expressing the view that the public was awakening gradually to the real meaning for America of Howells' essays. Walker remarked further that he believed the story in book form would sell widely and become a classic. Indeed, wrote Walker in his next letter, he would like to publish "A Traveller From Altruria" as a book, edited either by himself alone or with Howells.[24] Howells was saying the right thing to the country, which was in a critical condition.[25] Of this Walker was so confident that he engaged Howells to write a second series of Altrurian essays for *The Cosmopolitan* to begin the month following the conclusion of the first series.[26]

In the *New York Herald* for Sunday, September 3, 1893,[27] there appeared a two-and-a-half-column article describing Walker's meteoric rise to fame. The article, accompanied by a double-column drawing of the handsome Walker poring over a pile of books and manuscripts, was appropriately captioned "Napoleon of the Magazine World," with the subtitle, "John Brisben Walker Begins a

Revolution in the Publishing of Periodical Literature." After tracing Walker's career and describing his "keen brown eyes," which glanced out under "powerful brows," there followed a description of that "restless, inquiring, commanding" personality which suggested why Howells withdrew from too close an association:

> Mr. Walker dominates and moves the whole establishment like an electric current. He will accept and carry out a good suggestion from a wandering beggar and he will throw aside a bad suggestion from the highest literary authority.

Since one can well imagine that Howells himself might occasionally have been that "highest literary authority" whose suggestions were summarily thrown aside, one admires even more the fact that Howells managed to stay in a working relation to Walker long after he had severed his editorial position. The unidentified writer of the *Herald* article summed up Howells' connection with Walker in September, 1893, as follows:

> Mr. Walker's principal literary advisers and friends are Mr. Howells and Mr. Boyesen. Two years ago he secured Mr. Howells as editor of his magazine at a salary of virtually $15,-000 a year. But Mr. Howells hated the routine and wanted to get back to authorship. He gets $5,000 a year now and writes one article for each number.

Howells continued to write his article a month on the observations of Aristides Homos for still another year, for the Altrurian's comments on strikes, trade unions, the status of workers, deserted farms, and kindred subjects continued to fill Howells' mind even when he happened to be spending a few weeks in a New Hampshire hotel. Though Mr. Twelvemough had earned a vacation, Mr. Homos hardly allowed him to relax.

A letter to C. E. Norton, of July 10, 1892, makes one realize that for the time at least, Aristides Homos had taken the place of Mr. Twelvemough in Howells' imagination. Howells, as the writer of annual novels himself, usually found material in a summer hotel for another deftly turned romance. But that year, he wrote Norton, the hotel had not "the young gaiety" of the year before. Instead, he lamented, "we have an excursion of eighty Massachusettes Assessors, many in linen dusters." How could one "get that feeling into fiction"—of "the curious passivity and blankness of an American crowd?" The only "interesting people" on whom Howells could report were "a Dutch lady with her two sons." She, with a "continental simplicity" amusing to Howells, talked with him of "her father's family pride, and how he wished them all to keep up the barriers of race and nobility. 'But that is ridiculous, you know!' she said, as if the notion had not occurred to me before—Otherwise the place is not so distracting as to take my mind off my story a great deal." [28]

Was the story Howells referred to in his letter to Norton "A Traveller From Altruria," by Aristides Homos, or was it "The Coast of Bohemia" by Mr. Twelvemough? As we shall see in the next chapter, Howells was working on both of these "romances" intermittently during that summer and the following autumn and winter, for he was, in spite of himself, both the Traveler and the popular novelist, Mr. Twelvemough.

NOTES

1. The *New York Daily Tribune* carried the front-page story on July 1, 1892, "The Homestead Works Closed." The next day came the full story, "A Day of Rioting," p. 1. Stories and editorial comment filled the columns of the paper during July, 1892.

2. *Life in Letters*, II, pp. 24–25. Howells commented further on the Homestead strike in Letter I of "Letters of an Altrurian Traveller," *The Cosmopolitan*, XVI–XVII (November, 1893), pp. 110–111. See *Letters of an Altrurian Traveller* by William Dean Howells. Edited by Clara M. Kirk and Rudolf Kirk. Scholars' Facsimiles & Reprints, 1961. Pp. 13–14.

3. *Life in Letters*, II, 12.

4. July 24, 1892. *Life in Letters*, II, p. 26.

5. Pp. 572–575.

6. P. 1.

7. See "A Hazard of New Fortunes," *Harper's Weekly*, XXXIII (Oct. 10, 1889), p. 830. Compare Howells' remark in a letter to Garland, "Annie Kilburn is from first to last a cry for justice not alms." *Life in Letters*, I, p. 419.

8. *The Cosmopolitan*, XIV (February, 1893), pp. 495–498. *A Traveler*, pp. 69–89.

9. *Idem.*, XV (July, 1893), pp. 309–310. *A Traveler*, p. 229.

10. Howells to his father, July 10, 1892. *Life in Letters*, II, p. 25.

11. *The Cosmopolitan*, XIV (December, 1892), p. 251. *A Traveler*, p. 26. Cf. Murat Halstead, "Adirondack Forests," in "Current Events," *The Cosmopolitan* (July, 1891), p. 376.

12. *Idem.* (April, 1893), pp. 704–705. *A Traveler*, pp. 145–146.

13. *Idem.*, XV (May, 1893), p. 39. *A Traveler*, pp. 149–151. Howells was also aware of the fact that one of Walker's many social concerns was the plight of the American farmer. Soon after the purchase of *The Cosmopolitan*, Walker had offered two prizes of $400 each, one for the best essay by the daughter of

a farmer, "descriptive of farm life, with suggestions as to ways of making farm life attractive and happy"; the other for the best article by a farmer on "the needs of the farmer, his hours of labor, and the national legislation necessary for his prosperity." The subject, Walker observed, "is a most interesting one, and of vital importance to the welfare of the country." The two articles appeared in the April and June, 1891, issues of the magazine, and supplied Howells with first-hand material on the discomforts, frustrations, and suffering of country folk for which he found ample illustration in his walks around his own New Hampshire hotel.

While "A Traveler" was still appearing in *The Cosmopolitan*, Clifton Johnson's article, "The Deserted Homes of New England" came out in the June, 1893, issue of the magazine.

14. "A New Observer," *Atlantic Monthly*, XLV (June, 1880), 848–849. Jonathan Baxter Harrison (1835–1907) was a Unitarian minister, born in Ohio, and ordained in 1860. His home was in Franklin Falls, New Hampshire.

15. February 19, 1893. *Life in Letters*, II, p. 34. Harrison's contacts with Howells are discussed by Olov W. Fryckstedt, *In Quest of America, A Study of Howells' Early Development as a Novelist* (1958). For a history of the effort to preserve the New Hampshire forests between 1880 and 1903, see Charles D. Smith, "The Mountain Lover Mourns," *New England Quarterly*, XXXIII (March, 1960), 37–56.

16. *Observations on the Treatment of Public Plantations* (1889), a Report on Central Park, New York.

17. Pp. 306–307.

18. In *The Cosmopolitan* from 1892 to 1894, Walker featured a series of articles on "Great American Railways," written by railroad men. Walker thought that railways had seen their best days. When he described the transportation exhibit at the Columbian Exposition in Chicago in 1893, he concluded with a plea for government ownership. "It is an hour of change. No one can possibly predict what the future contains, and railroad properties . . . may become almost useless." *The Cosmopolitan*, XV (September, 1893), 590.

19. P. 104. Howells wrote, in his unpublished Notebooks, concerning the Traveler from Altruria, "Sometimes seems wholly subjective, like one's own consciousness of better things. Bring this idea in towards the end." The Notebook is now being

edited by George Arms. The above quotation is printed with the permission of Professor W. W. Howells.

20. *The Critic*, XIX (January 14, 1893), 22.
21. *The Cosmopolitan*, XV (May, 1893), 41. *A Traveler*, p. 160.
22. March 13, 1893. John Brisben Walker to Howells. Unpublished letter. Houghton Library, Harvard.
23. *Idem.*, March 30, 1893.
24. *Idem.*, April, 1893.
25. *Idem.*, August 20, 1893.
26. "Letters of an Altrurian Traveller," *The Cosmopolitan*, XVI–XVII, November, 1893–September, 1894.
27. P. 13.
28. Manuscript letter. Houghton Library, Harvard.

Chapter IV

Greece and Bohemia
New York, 1892–1893

Howells and his wife returned to New York in the autumn of 1892, this time to an apartment overlooking Central Park.[1] Something of his relief in finding himself away from the old surroundings of Stuyvesant Square is felt in the letter Howells wrote to his Boston friend, Charles E. Norton, on October 16, 1892:

> We are sinking into such quiet as we can find in this hurly-burly, and I am getting my old books about me again, out of the boxes where they have been shut up for five years.

These precious books, which Howells had not held in his hands since 1887—since, indeed, before his earlier stay in New York—plunged his thoughts into his still more remote past. As he remarked to Norton concerning the little volumes:

> Most of them are pangs, wounds from the past, with its manifold associations, and its power to hurt. What a grotesque notion, that anyone should be willing to live his life over again.[2]

Painful though it might have been for Howells "to live his life over again" through a renewed acquaintance with his library, he nevertheless found in this experience the

75

nourishment he needed for his intensely literary mental life. Rearranging the books of his youth on the shelves of his new apartment threw Howells into a reflective state of mind concerning the two important pieces of writing on which he had been working during the summer, "The Coast of Bohemia" and "A Traveller From Altruria." [3] These serials, which were soon to appear almost simultaneously in two popular magazines,[4] reflect in a peculiar way the conflict of aim in Howells' mind in the summer and autumn of 1892, a conflict which grew more marked as he turned over the pages of the books which he had not seen for five years. As the autumn wore on, Howells found it increasingly laborious to bring "The Coast of Bohemia" to a conclusion; his interest in "A Traveller From Altruria," however, grew as he thumbed through his favorite authors, especially Goldsmith.

That the conflict was real is apparent from Howells' comments to friends and family during these months. In the same letter to Norton from which we have just quoted, Howells wrote concerning "The Coast of Bohemia,"

I am working hard on a story, which is behaving very ungratefully, and making very little return for my trouble; and I ask myself very serious questions about my power and fitness to go on in the line I have kept so long.

Two months later, on December 11, 1892, he again wrote to Norton about the tiresome story:

To-day I finished the story which has been lagging so long, and I think I have ended an epoch of my literary life. I doubt if I shall ever write another story in which mating and marrying plays an important part. I am too old for it, and it does not interest me.[5]

The following month Howells wrote to his old Cambridge friend, Mrs. Annie T. Fields, the widow of his former superior on the *Atlantic*, to thank her for an essay she had written on Whittier. Here, he casually remarked, "I displease myself with everything I write," and ended his note with the whimsical observation that "there is one advantage of being in New York, however; if I have stopped thinking, I can console myself that it is because I am here." [6]

Several weeks later, Howells' divided and dissatisfied mind was cheered by "the little package of books" sent from his home in Jefferson, Ohio, by his father. Howells needed the sight and feel of his old library to help him relive his "Literary Passions"—the title he gave the new series of essays to which he had, in the fall of 1892,[7] turned his mind. By glancing into Goldsmith's *History of Greece* —for that is what the package contained—Howells revived his lagging spirits and thus was able to enrich the essays on Altruria, already beginning to appear in *The Cosmopolitan*. Howells' pleasure in handling the two volumes which he had read and reread as a boy is reflected in his letter to his father, February 19, 1893:

The little package of books came safely and promptly, and I am exceedingly glad to have them. I am greatly surprised to find that the *History of Greece* is in two volumes; I had always remembered it in one, and had spoken of it so in what I had already written. I now wish you would send me the bundle of scraps that you mention; any helps to my memory will be very useful; the letters I do not care for. I am getting on very rapidly with the work, and I hope to be through with the whole twelve papers ["My Literary Passions"] by the end of March. Of course, it is a kind of thing that could be indefinitely extended, but unless it is to include the whole story of my life, it may as well stop at one place as another.[8]

That the whole story of Howells' life might be told in terms of his "literary passions" is clear to those who open this literary autobiography. Chapter II, for example, is entitled "Goldsmith," and here, Howells tells us, that it seemed to him, "in the sharply foreshortened perspective of the past," that he read Cervantes, Irving, and Goldsmith, all at once. But of the three, Goldsmith came first in the pleasure given him. "He came so early that I cannot tell when or where I began to read him, but it must have been before I was ten years old." Of the books recently sent him by his father, Howells wrote:

I do not know in the least how Goldsmith's *Greece* came into my hands, though I fancy it must have been procured for me because of a taste which I showed for that kind of reading, and I can imagine no greater luck for a small boy in a small town of Southwestern Ohio well-nigh fifty years ago. I have the books yet; two little, stout volumes in fine print, with the marks of wear on them.[9]

There were some cherry trees in the Howells yard, "and in one of them there was a level branch where a boy could sit with a book till his dangling legs went to sleep, or till some idler or busier boy came to the gate and called him down to play marbles or go swimming." Then "the ancient world was rolled up like a scroll, and put away until the next day, with all its orators and conspirators, its nymphs and satyrs, gods and demigods; though sometimes they escaped at night and got into the boy's dreams."

The dreams stirred again in Howells' mind in the early winter of 1892, as he stood by his apartment window and looked across the trees in Central Park. How precisely the overtones of Goldsmith's *History of Greece* wove themselves among many other threads into the fabric of "A Traveller From Altruria," one cannot, of course, say. One can, however, point out that the device of Howells' literary adventure—new to his pen, but not new as a device—reminds one at once of Goldsmith's *Citizen of the World.* Here a traveler from a far land, in this case China, comments ironically to his friends at home on the civilization of London; Goldsmith's purpose, like that of Howells more than a century later, was to make the scales drop from the eyes of his contemporaries. Howells was "passionately" devoted to Goldsmith from his boyhood:

I was not consciously his admirer till I began to read, when I was fourteen, a little volume of his essays, made up, I dare say, from the *Citizen of the World* and other unsuccessful ventures of his.

Howells himself then tried to write sketches and stories after the manner of Goldsmith, for "I have never greatly loved an author without trying to write like him." It was some time, Howells confessed, before he found it best to be as like himself as he could, no matter how deeply "in love" with his master he was. Certainly Howells had long since learned to write, think, speak in his own voice when he opened again his Goldsmith volumes. Yet it is rather startling to hear Howells observe in 1892—reflecting on the literary emotions of more than fifty years earlier, and especially those he had for Goldsmith—that "the adoration which a young writer has for a great one is truly a passion passing the love of women."

Since Howells' reading habits were "desultory," he could not recall the order in which "The Deserted Village," *The Vicar of Wakefield*, and Goldsmith's own tale of *The Traveler* became a part of his literary stream of consciousness. The memory of his father reading aloud the poetry of Goldsmith came back to him as he unpacked his books and arranged them around his study shelves. *The Vicar of Wakefield*, which he had read several times already and hoped to read many times more, was still for him "one of the most modern novels; that is to say, one of the best." Goldsmith's kindness, his lack of arrogance, made him for Howells, a "contemporary." These are the qualities which mark the style of the author of "A Traveller From Altruria," who displeased himself with everything he wrote in the fall and winter of 1892–1893, until he found his way back to his earlier "passion" for the classical world.[10]

Though Howells frequently returned to his own past by rereading his favorite authors, he nonetheless lived fully in the present during this winter in New York. In his letter of January 22, 1893, to his father we are reminded of Howells' interest in the current social problems of his day by the brief reference to two old friends and associates of the last decade in Boston. "Hamlin Garland is coming to supper with us, this evening, and then he and I are going to Henry George's for the evening," [11] he wrote with satisfaction. Henry George lived a block or two from Howells' former home on Stuyvesant Square and Howells and enjoyed dropping in on the older man when they had been neighbors. Without much effort of the imagination one can accompany Garland and Howells down Fifty-ninth Street to Fifth Avenue, then board a horse-drawn bus to Union Square and walk to the home of the elderly George. He was described by Howells to his father as "a short, stout little man, not quite my bulk, and very fair," who "liked a good laugh nearly as well as I did." [12]

The author of *Progress and Poverty* would have had much to discuss with the author of "A Traveller From Altruria," especially when he came for an evening of talk accompanied by Garland, one of the editors of *The Dawn*. This outspoken periodical had served, since 1889, as a platform for the ideas of Henry George, as well as those of

Gronlund, Bellamy, Tolstoy, Ely, and many others concerned with the pressing social problems of the day.[13] Such an evening must have renewed Howells' memory of the two years he spent in Boston associating with the Christian Socialists and the Nationalists. For though Howells had at this time transferred his home to New York, he maintained "a kind of passionate interest in Boston," which, said Howells, "belongs distinctively to the minor capitals like Athens and Florence."[14] Furthermore, he observed, thinking of the men and women he had met there, "It is full of social suggestion, and I think it is the most open-minded place in the country."[15] A well-ordered urban civilization suggested to Howells' mind the ancient cities of Greece and Italy, as well as the concepts of Christian Socialism.

The social problems of the ancient world, as described by Goldsmith, Howells saw, too, reflected in the sprawling metropolis where he had come to live. Goldsmith's description of Sparta, for example, might serve for a comment on New York at the beginning of the depression of the 1890's:

The generality of the people were at that time so poor, that they were destitute of every kind of possession, whilst a small number of individuals were possessed of all the lands and the wealth of the country.

Lycurgus' solution brings us near that remote but real land of Altruria where Howells' imagination felt at home:

In order, therefore, to banish the insolence, the fraud, and the luxury of the one, as well as the misery, the repining, and the factious despair of the others, he persuaded the majority, and forced the rest to give up all their lands to the commonwealth, and to make a new division of them, that they might all live together in perfect equality.[16]

In Chapter III of *The History of Greece*, Goldsmith described "the Government of Athens, the Laws of Solon, and the History of the Republic from the Time of Solon to the Commencement of the Persian War," suggesting to Howells several of the basic concepts which fall so smoothly from the lips of Aristides Homos, our Altrurian. The most important among these was that of the vote. Solon, wrote Goldsmith,

gave every private citizen a privilege of voting in the great assembly of the whole body of the state. This, indeed, at first might appear a concession of small consequence, but it was soon found to contain very solid advantages; for, by the laws of Athens, it was permitted, after the determination of the magistrates, to appeal to the general assembly of the people, and thus in time, all causes of weight and moment came before them.

To turn over the leaves of Goldsmith's *History of Greece* is to find oneself in the very atmosphere of Altruria over which played the winds of Attica as well as those of Jerusalem. As the professor in "A Traveller From Altruria" listened to Mr. Homos' description of Altruria, he leaned over to the banker and whispered, "A little hint from Sparta," [17] for he, too, recognized the interplay of Christian and Grecian thought in the Traveler's speech. One is reminded by Goldsmith, as Howells must have been similarly reminded, that democracy stems, not only from the early Christians but also from the Athenians, who believed that a mind "obliged to take part in public concerns, learns, from habit, to make those concerns its principal care, and self-interest quickly sinks before them." [18] The concept of altruism meant the sinking of self in the interest of the group. Though the Christians stressed brotherhood and the Athenians civic justice, the final aim of both was closely related and became harmoniously fused in the mind of Howells as he reread the volumes sent to him by his father. The answer to "the misfortunes of the public" of New York in 1893, as well as of Athens in the time of Solon, was to be sought in juster laws for all; "justice, not alms," was the "charity" really desired by the poor.[19]

It is worth reflecting that the name of the Altrurian was Aristides Homos. The phrase "Aristides the Just" comes at once to the reader's mind, and also the fact that "homos" implies "common man" or Man in the abstract. The Traveler, then, was the "just" man, who, though "common," carried with him something of the renown of the actual Athenian general, Aristides, who had advocated a peaceful and conservative policy; he was, nevertheless, the military hero of Marathon when the Persians threatened the safely of this non-belligerent state. Athens, the city of Aristides, was regarded by Goldsmith as the cradle of our civil liberties. In *Years of My Youth*,[20] Howells wrote of himself as a boy of eleven: "The truth is I was preoccupied . . . with the politics of Rome and Athens, as I conceived them from the ever-dear histories of Goldsmith"; in rereading these same volumes as an elderly man, he was reminded that we owe to Greece our national tradition of "life, liberty, and the pursuit of happiness."

With these overtones, both Christian and pagan, in one's mind, one turns to Howells' November, 1892, contribution to *The Cosmopolitan*, with an enlivened understanding of the social questions discussed by Aristides Homos and Mr. Twelvemough, the weary writer of serial stories for current magazines. These prove to be the very questions that were uppermost in the minds of the men and women who formed the group of Christian Socialists in Boston during Howells' sojourn there between 1889 and 1891. The immediate reason for the appearance of this series of twelve essays commenting on the disturbances of the period was the aggressive policy of John Brisben Walker, the new editor-owner of *The Cosmopolitan*. Howells had found he could not work in day-to-day contact with Walker, though his social aims offered Howells, he had thought at the time, a chance to respond to the appeal of Bliss to all writers for stronger expressions of their reforming programs. Finally, the serene and rather remote atmosphere of Altruria came to Howells, after a summer in New Hampshire, straight from the eighteenth century, where as a boy Howells had dreamed away much of his time under the guidance of the free spirit of Goldsmith, who understood the relationship of wealth, poverty, and the vote, in terms which deeply affected the American dream of this novelist-turned-reformer. Howells sought refuge in Altruria when he no longer saw any hope in Egoria, the selfish world of unrestricted competition.

"The Coast of Bohemia," which Howells was writing at the same time that he was working on "A Traveller From Altruria" gives one the impression that it was written by Mr. Twelvemough. In "A Traveller From Altruria," however, Howells becomes Mr. Homos. Here this successful journalist-novelist, with socialistic leanings, found himself engaged in a serious and faintly humourous argument with himself, in the course of which he brought to bear his Christian yearnings and his tempered classicism on the current problems of poverty and suffering in the midst of profligate wealth. Soon after their publication as books, these two romances were reviewed together in *The Atlantic Monthly* of November, 1894, under the heading, "America, Altruria, and the Coast of Bohemia." According to his *Atlantic* critic, Howells

Howells at work in "The Barnbury," the barn converted into his workshop at his summer home in Kittery Point, Maine

A bomb exploding during the Anarchist (Haymarket) Riot in Chicago. Wood engraving by T. de Thulstrup after H. Jeanneret, 1886

On the Midway at The Columbian Exposition (World's Fair), Chicago, 189

The Court of Honor at The Columbian Exposition. In the foreground visitor are observing one of the electric fountains, seen for the first time at "The Whit City"

The defeated Pinkerton men (foreground) about to leave the scene of the riot at the Carnegie Iron and Steel Company, Homestead, Pennsylvania. Drawing by W. P. Snyder after a photograph by Dabbs (Pittsburgh) taken in 1892

Henry Mills Alden, editor of
Harper's Monthly Magazine
Culver Pictures

John Brisben Walker, owner-
editor of *The Cosmopolitan*
Brown Brothers

has preserved his mental balance and his realism, in true Utopian manner by turning from the thoughts which have filled his mind in these latter years to the production of a novel like *The Coast of Bohemia*, a piece of light literature, very much in his earlier manner, but in no discord with any later thought.

Which was "the real Howells," Mr. Twelvemough or Mr. Homos? A reader of today might ask the same question as did the critic of 1894. Mr. Twelvemough, in "A Traveller From Altruria," voiced Howells' own suspicion that Mr. Homos was only an "idea," when he admitted to a very uneasy feeling as he observed the Traveler on the hotel porch in New Hampshire:

I glanced at the Altrurian, sitting attentive and silent, and a sudden misgiving crossed my mind concerning him. Was he really a man, a human entity, a personality like ourselves, or was he merely a sort of spiritual solvent, sent for a moment to precipitate whatever sincerity there was in us, and show us what the truth was concerning our relations to each other? [21]

"Human entity" or "spiritual solvent," Aristides Homos possessed sufficient vitality to deepen Howells' insight into the problems of his day and to make him turn with weariness from Mr. Twelvemough's latest romance, "The Coast of Bohemia." The writer of annual novels was bored by his own serial; he found himself more deeply absorbed by "A Traveller From Altruria." Mr. Homos became for Howells at this time "really a man," while Mr. Twelvemough grew increasingly more shadowy.

After Howells' Altrurian essays appeared in book form in 1894, their meaning for America gripped the imagination of a wide circle of readers. Why should not America make real the dream of Altruria? John Brisben Walker confided to Howells that he himself was secretly writing "A

Brief History of Altruria." [22] In the November, 1895, issue of *The Cosmopolitan* appeared an article entitled "The Discovery of Altruria," supposedly written by Sir Robert Harton, an African explorer who had recently come to New York to supervise his investments. "After a hard day's work," Sir Robert purchased a copy of *The Cosmopolitan* at the Brevoort House, returned to his room and "soon became interested in the experiences of the Altrurian Traveler contributed to that magazine by Mr. W. D. Howells." Sir Robert "sat in reverie for some minutes" after he had read Howells' essay, for he was reminded of the story told him by an Arab chief with whom he had once camped in the Upper Congo. Convinced that Virland, the remote area of Africa described by the Arab was, in fact, Altruria, Sir Robert (whose investments were not prospering) determined to organize an expedition to discover "the real Altruria." Sir Robert applied immediately to the editor of *The Cosmopolitan* for financial support, and this was promptly granted him. In the next issue of the magazine [23] "A Brief History of Altruria" began; it was compiled, we are told in a footnote, at the capital of Altruria by Sir Robert Harton, under the direction and with the assistance of Moi-Nol-Fay, one of the governors of Virland, from the histories and records of that country." According to these records, Virland was settled in 1642, by Dutch and English settlers who were thrown ashore in Africa when on their way to Virginia. They brought with them the Christian religion, established a settlement on Christian principles, erected public buildings with Corinthian columns, and were thriving in a simple way, until the mid-nineteenth century, when a handful of Americans arrived, bringing science and inventions. This "enlightenment" led to the accumulation of wealth, which was accompanied by fierce competition, and general corruption. At last the people were moved to bring about a bloodless revolution and to establish their society on the theory that "the highest political economy was to take care of one's neighbor." Now in Virland, Sir Robert reported, "the law of Christ has become synonymous with the law of the land." At the close of the fourth and last chapter of "A Brief History," a "Note by the Editor" placed the question before the reader: "How can mankind work out an ideal which would be scientific in its distribution and embody in its fullest extent the ideas first presented in the teachings of Jesus Christ, and lastly in the declaration of human right subscribed to by the American colonists?" Thus Walker reworded for his readers the essential ideas of Howells' Altrurian philosophy.

That Howells' concept of an Altrurian America, firmly based on Christian brotherhood, modified by Grecian intelligence, took root in his time is further attested by the appearance of two books in 1895, *Altruria*, by Titus K. Smith, and *God in His World*, by Henry Mills Alden. The first of these books was so obviously inspired by *A Traveler From Altruria* that Alden wrote to Howells asking him whether he considered it worth his while to sue the author.[24] The second, by Howells' old and trusted friend, simply suggested that Alden and Howells shared with many writers of the period a hope for Christianity as a social force. They must have discussed the interplay of Christian and Grecian thought which, according to both writers, underlies American civilization.

Titus K. Smith dedicated his book "To all who are hoping and working for the progress of humanity, longing for the fullness of liberty and social reason, whose dawn only we now enjoy." Whether or not Smith intended a pun on the magazine, *The Dawn,* we cannot say; certainly, when John Optimus explains to his friend, Sam Wheeler, "I am not a socialist, but an Altruist," [25] we feel we are back in the old atmosphere. Altruria, in this case, proves to be an actual town between St. Paul and Minneapolis, where the small homes, equipped with electric lights and telephones, are owned by the Altrurian Corporation. Central kitchens make servants unnecessary; farming and manufacturing, sufficient to maintain the community, leave plenty of time for hymns and songs in the evening. Wagons of light steel, propelled by gas engines, move along well-paved roads lined with trees and flowers. Money, "merely the tool of exchange," is not an incentive in Altruria, where all work from religious conviction. "In fact, no one can be an Altrurian who is not a real Christian. . . . We Altrurians also never work for ourselves, to gain for self as much as possible, but we serve each other." [26] There is but one Church, which is Catholic—an *American* Catholic Church, John hastily explains, "not a Roman Catholic Church, but Catholic in the sense that your 'Church of the Strangers' in New York had the true spirit of catholicity." [27] Smith's account of social classes, taxes, dress, the vote, must have made Howells realize, if ever he doubted it, what an effective teacher he was.

Alden's book, *God in His World,* described an Altruria of the spirit, and had nothing to do with model homes, electricity, or costume. It was, the author announced, "A Christian interpretation of the Glorious period of Hellenic civilization, especially that of the first three centuries." If only the "simplicity of the early Aryan faith" had survived in Greece, "there would have been shown on the shores and among the islands of the Aegean as wondrous an example of spiritual as we now behold of aesthetic and intellectual development." [28] Alden directed his readers to the very section of the world where Howells had located the land of Altruria. Alden, however, attempted to lead his readers back through history: "After the Imperial adoption of Christianity, and during its long Roman sepulture in the Middle Ages, we shall see that there is a real Christendom under its ecclesiastical mask—that the Christian embodiment in human fellowship still goes on, since it is God and not the church that takes care of the kingdom." Guided more by vision than by history, Alden was soon caught up by "the accelerated movement of modern times" where we "spiritually discern only the divine quickening of the Brotherhood, while even yet this fellowship is not visible as an outward embodiment." Alden, too, dreamed of a "divine human fellowship," [29] an ideal society, in which all labor alike, where there is time for play as well as work, and where there is the minimum of government, and brotherhood has replaced competition.

With these three well-meaning imitators of Howells we bring to a conclusion this chapter of our study of how ideas—in this instance Christian and classical—fused in Howells' mind during a particularly creative period in his life and how they were reconsidered in the light of the social injustices of his times. After two years in Boston and six months on *The Cosmopolitan*, Howells had surprised his readers again by presenting to them "A Traveller From Altruria." "I see you are drawing a longish bow in the Cosmopolitan," [30] James wrote to Howells from his perch in London, after the first several essays had appeared. In a sense, "A Traveller From Altruria" was the longest bow Howells was ever to draw, for his aim was directed at America, and his arrow hit the mark.

Others, besides Howells, were eager to put their faith

in "progress," conceived in Christian and neoclassical terms. No more tangible expression of this dream could be presented than the Chicago Columbian Exposition, just then being erected on the shores of Lake Michigan. Here the Traveler journeyed, when his New Hampshire summer came to an end, to study at first hand an American version of Altruria, built on the outposts of Egoria.

NOTES

1. 40 West 59th Street, New York City. Here Howells lived from October, 1892, to April, 1896.
2. *Life in Letters*, II, 27.
3. See George Arms, "Howells's Unpublished Prefaces," *New England Quarterly*, XVII (November–December, 1944), 587–591.
4. "The Coast of Bohemia" was published in *The Ladies' Home Journal* from December, 1892 through October, 1893. The book was troublesome to Howells from the start, although, he wrote, "the story ran glibly from the point of my pen" ("Unpublished Prefaces," p. 589). Edward Bok, editor of *The Ladies Home Journal*, engaged Howells for $5,000 to write a 50,000 word "story for girls" in January, 1891. However, he was not satisfied with the first installment and insisted on a revision by Howells. When it finally appeared, Howells resented the fact that it was "tampered with" by the editor. See manuscript letters from Bok to Howells, dated January 9, 1891, January 21, 1891, and October 5, 1892. Houghton Library, Harvard. "A Traveller From Altruria" came out in *The Cosmopolitan* between November, 1892, and October, 1893.
5. *Life in Letters*, II, 29.
6. *Idem.*, January 21, 1893, pp. 30–31.
7. These essays were published in *The Ladies' Home Journal*

between December, 1893, and March, 1895. They were issued in book form in October, 1895.

8. *Life in Letters*, II, 33.

9. See also Waldon Fawcett, "Mr. Howells and His Brother," *The Critic*, XXXII (November, 1899), 1027. Here Fawcett reports that Howells' brother told him that William "took special delight" in Goldsmith's *History of Greece*. Mildred Howells stated, "It must have been in Hamilton that he read Goldsmith's *Greece*." (*Life in Letters*, I, 4.)

10. *My Literary Passions* (1895), Chapter II. It is a curious fact that when "A Traveller From Altruria" appeared in book form in 1894, the spelling had been altered to *Traveler*. Perhaps the change in the spelling of the word was a part of Howells' "war" on modern English ways and habits. In the "Editor's Study" of November, 1891, he warned his readers that it might be time to rebel against England once more; in which case, "we notify them that not only will the American parlance become the English language, but it will be spelled according to Noah Webster," and that "the 'traveller' will have to limp along on one *l*."

11. *Life in Letters*, II, 31.

12. *Idem.* (July 20, 1892), p. 21. For the effect of George's ideas on the single tax on Howells' "Traveller From Altruria," see W. F. Taylor, "On the Origin of Howells' Interest in Economic Reform," *op. cit.*

13. See, for instance, Ezra P. Gould, "Henry George or Edward Bellamy; Which or Neither?" *The Dawn* (June, 1890), pp. 53–65. The points stressed in this article were those familiar to the whole group of writers for *The Dawn*: "The evil in the present social state is the unequal distribution of property." What is the remedy? "The regeneration of the human heart through Christ" (p. 53). The opening paragraph of an essay by Richard T. Ely, "The Nature and Significance of Corporations," reflects the thought of the Christian Socialists with whom Ely was associated. Ely's essay appeared in *Harper's*, LXXIV (May, 1887), 970–977, soon after Howells joined the staff. Ely wrote, in words which might have been spoken by the Altrurian himself, "Our age is more democratic than other ages because it is more Christian. This significance of the mighty onward strides of democracy, so often overlooked, becomes manifest when we consider the essential nature of the

social message which the great Founder of Christianity brought to our race. What does Christianity mean to the student of social science? It means the brotherhood of man, because it means the fatherhood of God. In this is implied the trite phrase, 'A man and his brother,' so full of meaning to him who has comprehended it. All men are brothers; then all men have certain equal rights, and among them is the right of self-development. . . . What a glorious thing, then, is this triumph of democracy! It means that we are approaching nearer to the purpose for which humanity exists." See also Howells' reviews of Laurence Gronlund's *Ça Ira* and *Co-operative Common-wealth, Harper's*, LXXVI (April, 1888), 801–802.

14. See the "Editor's Study," *Harper's*, LXXIV (May, 1887), 986. After discussing the intolerance of Puritans of New England, Howells reviewed two anonymous books: *Day in Athens with Socrates* and *Talks with Socrates about Life*. These books made clear "what an intolerable nuisance wisdom and goodness must be to most respectable people. Here was a man who, by his own showing and the showing of all the witnesses of his life, dwelt in lasting poverty in order that he might have time to be wise and truly great; and not only this, but he spent the greater part of his vast leisure in going about and convincing some of the leading citizens, who had always supposed themselves wise and truly great, that they were really nothing of the kind. The religious state of the ancient Athens bore with Socrates a very long time; but we know what end he came to at last, and we feel sure that the religious state of the nascent modern Athens would have made much shorter work with him. He seems, like the Quakers, to have thought himself guilty of no wrong, and in his conscious innocence he refused to put himself beyond the jurisdiction of the worshipful magistrates and ministers; he escaped whipping at the cart's tail through Ipswich, Salem, and other towns, but he was put to death at last.

"Was it on Boston Common? Not exactly, we believe; but there is an effect of something so recent, such an essential parity in all stories of human cruelty and folly, that we might well be excused a slight confusion of details. The little books themselves are somewhat to blame. That *Day in Athens with Socrates*, those *Talks with Socrates about Life*, and that first volume containing the Apology and the Phaedo, all strike a note so familiar, deal with questions so living, that they seem of present concern and of modern fact."

15. "An Hour With Howells," *op. cit.*, p. 118, col. 2.

16. Oliver Goldsmith, *The History of Greece*, I (1809), 21. Compare Hamlin Garland, "The Cause of Poverty," *The Dawn*, June 15, 1889. Compare also "American Millionaires: Origin of Their Fortunes," *New York Tribune*, Sunday, June 5, 1892, Pt. II, p. 13. See also, W. D. Howells, "Are We a Plutocracy?" *North American Review*, CLVIII (February, 1894), 185–196.

17. *The Cosmopolitan*, XV (October, 1893), 742. *A Traveler*, p. 294.

18. Goldsmith, p. 51. Howells was, in the fall of 1892, also reading for the first time Renan's *Life of Christ*, which, he wrote to Norton, he considered sentimental. "Such corrosive things since!" he added. *Life in Letters*, II, 29.

19. *Life in Letters*, I, 419.

20. P. 27. Aristides, an Athenian general and statesman, surnamed "The Just," who commanded his tribe at the battle of Marathon (490 B.C.) and was archon in 489 B.C. He was the advocate of a quiet and conservative policy as opposed to the "strong navy" policy of Themistocles. He died in 483 B.C., so poor that his funeral could not be paid for from his estate.

21. *The Cosmopolitan*, XV (May, 1893), 44. *A Traveler*, p. 172.

22. October 29, 1895. Unpublished letter. Houghton Library, Harvard.

23. *The Cosmopolitan*, XX, November, 1895–March, 1896.

24. Unpublished letter of Alden to Howells in Houghton Library, Harvard. See Louis J. Budd, *op. cit.* Introduction, footnote 3. I am indebted to Mr. Budd for his citation of the books of Alden and Smith, as well as for his reference to the Altrurian articles by Walker in *The Cosmopolitan*.

25. *Altruria*, p. 18.

26. *Idem.*, p. 36.

27. *God in His World*, p. 41. "Church of the Stranger" suggests "Church of the Carpenter."

28. *Idem.*, p. 49. For Howells' view of Alden, and especially for Howells' comment on *God in His World*, see "In Memoriam," *Harper's*, CXL (December, 1919), 133–136.

29. *God in His World*, pp. 187–188. For an account by Alden of the writing of this book, see *The House of Harper, op. cit.*, pp. 419–420. In a letter addressed to the Right Reverend J. D.

Huntington, Alden thanked Huntington for his appreciative letter about his book addressed to a mutual friend. He then wrote, "Since 1862 I have been a member of the P. E. Church." *The House of Harper, op. cit.*, p. 599. Huntington was associated with R. Heber Newton in an attempt to establish a branch of the Church of the Carpenter in New York.

30. January 29, 1893. Unpublished letter. Houghton Library, Harvard.

Chapter V

The Columbian
Exposition
Chicago, 1893

Before "A Traveller From Altruria" came to a conclusion in the October, 1893, issue of *The Cosmopolitan*,
Aristides Homos had left the hills of New Hamsphire and
descended to New York. What precisely his plans for the
year were, or whom he was visiting in "Babylon"—the
Altrurian's name for New York—these facts are not re-
vealed by our Traveler. We know only that on September
1, 1893, he pulled out his writing pad and addressed to
his friend, Cyril, in Altruria, a long letter summing up his
thoughts on his first year in America. This fantastic country seemed to him, he wrote, "like a belated Altruria,
tardily repeating in the nineteenth century the errors
which we committed in the tenth." [1]

Before the month was ended, Homos wrote an even
longer letter to Cyril from Chicago describing the glories
of the World's Columbian Exposition of 1893, which he
had just visited. Aristides confessed that he had always
thought of Chicago as merely a sort of "ultimated Man-
hattan, the realized ideal of that largeness, loudness and

fastness, which New York has persuaded the Americans is metropolitan." Now, however, he felt that he had a vision of the possible future of this country which he must at once impart to Cyril:

. . . after seeing the World's Fair City here, I feel as if I had caught a glimpse of the glorious capitals which will whiten the hills and shores of the east and the borderless plains of the west, when the New York and the Newer New York of today shall seem to all the future Americans as impossible as they would seem to any Altrurian now.[2]

The eleven "Letters of an Altrurian Traveller," all addressed to Cyril, appeared, month by month, in *The Cosmopolitan* from November, 1893, to September, 1894, as a sequel to "A Traveller From Altruria." The last nine letters were concerned with the conditions in Babylon, where the Traveler found himself again after a "fortnight's stay in that vision of Altruria at the great Fair in Chicago." Returning to New York, he said, was like exposing himself "a second time to the shock of American conditions," now unsupported by the "romantic expectations" which buoyed him up on his first arrival. The weary Traveler confessed that he would like to take ship at once for his homeland and forget forever the harsh, competitive society of America. "But I have denied myself this," he wrote Cyril, "in the interest of the studies of plutocratic civilization which I wish to make." This high-minded purpose, however, could not lighten the burden which weighed down his spirits, for, as he wrote,

I had seen what might be, in the Fair City, and now I was to see again what the Americans say must be, in New York, and I shrank not only from the moral, but the physical ugliness of the thing.[3]

Whatever message Aristides wished to impart to Cyril, enjoying the enlightened civilization of far-off Altruria, is clearly Howells' own word on the America of his day addressed to his contemporaries. Howells himself paid a five-day visit to the Exposition in late September, 1893, as the guest of the Director, Daniel H. Burnham. This experience gave him the opportunity he needed to study the Chicago Exposition as an illustration of the Altrurian possibilities already existing in the American civilization. The remaining letters to Cyril are concerned with the effects of the competitive system on such a great center as New York City, both in terms of social wrongs and civic beauty. Long before our modern effort to contend with the problems of traffic, slum clearance, park systems, and crime, Howells was aware of these inevitable frustrations in a rapidly expanding individualistic society. The White City in Chicago vindicated his belief in co-operative solutions to these difficulties in the interest of all classes.

Immediately after the series came to an end in the September, 1894, issue of *The Cosmopolitan*, both the *New York Herald* and the *Daily Tribune* published articles in their Sunday editions,[4] pointing out that Howells' Altrurian thoughts were unmistakably socialistic in tone. The article in the *Herald* carried the caption "Poets Become Socialists Too," which was followed by the subtitle, "Howells Champions Socialism." He was, according to the unidentified writer, a socialist author of great importance; indeed,

perhaps the foremost champion of socialism among literary men of the present time is William Dean Howells. The novelist's entrance into the field of economics, holding a lance for unpopular doctrine, has been the cause of much surprise and mystification to his friends and admirers. Yet no one could read his novels, and particularly such as "A Hazard of New Fortunes" and "Silas Lapham," and even such a minor story as "The World of Chance" without realizing that the novelist has long been a serious student of such questions.

The article appearing in the *Daily Tribune* the following Sunday was a review of the book, *A Traveler From Altruria,* and bore the caption "Socialism Idealized." Howells, said the reviewer,

made the usual attempt to identify Socialism with Christianity, and quoted numerous passages of Scripture to support the claim, and studiously avoided all passages having an adverse bearing.

The reviewer was correct in concluding that Howells' approach to social problems when he was writing "A Traveller From Altruria" was basically that of the Christian Socialists. Howells' socialism remained Christian when he wrote his second Altrurian series the following year. However, after the Altrurian's visit to the Columbian Exposition, a new element—the classical—mingled with the familiar Christian tone.

The much-publicized Chicago Fair gave Howells the perfect example of socialism in action; his spokesman, Aristides Homos, recognized in the White City the very atmosphere of his homeland, for the buildings which rose from the swamps on the shores of Lake Michigan were the old American dream of the classic glory of Athens, as well as a hope for the industrial and cultural future of the United States. The December, 1893, issue of *The Cosmopolitan* contained the Altrurian's enthusiastic account of the Fair to his distant friend; his comments were a reflection of his—and Howells'—belief in democracy based on the fusion of Christian and classical civilization in the co-operative efforts of the New World. Howells' dream of an Altrurian America seemed to his generation distinctly radical in tone, though on closer examination it proves to be merely a reflection of the ideas of the Christian Socialists in the mind of a writer who had the good fortune to visit the White City.

That others besides Howells saw in the hundred and fifty classical buildings of the Fair, reflected in the waters of lakes and lagoons, a promise of the future is clear from the endless flow of illustrated articles that filled the magazines and the papers of the day. Francis Davis Millet, for example, as Director of Decorations,[5] wrote two magazine articles in the autumn of 1892 in which he commented upon the significance of the aesthetic theory behind the vast undertaking.[6] He predicted that the "grand style, the perfect proportions and the magnificent dimensions" of the buildings would mark "the renaissance of the true spirit of architecture in this country." He pointed out that the Director, David H. Burnham, had wisely adopted "a general classical style for all buildings," calling upon the united efforts of architects and artists from various parts of the country to forgo any attempts at originality in favor of the "immutable laws of harmony and proportion." It would be "worse than foolhardy to ask for originality," [7] Millet said; the importance of this demonstration that the architecture of Greece and Italy is firmly founded on "reason and common sense" adaptable to modern use, can "hardly be overestimated." The salutary influence of the Fair on "the future of architecture in this country can be prophesied with absolute certainty," Millet asserted. By the use of the new material of stucco, "which gleams like marble," the architects were enabled "to engage in an architectual spree"; they were free "to reproduce with fidelity and accuracy the best details of ancient architecture, to erect temples, colonnades, towers, and domes of surpassing beauty and of noble proportions." The fact that each building had "the complement of its architecture in sculpture and in painting" meant that the "allied arts" were seen for the first time in this country working together in harmonious accord. "It means the dawn of a real art in this country," concluded Millet, giving voice to the hopes of thousands who had contributed to the success of this internationally-acclaimed world exposition.

On March 25, 1893, after months of discouraging toil on the part of architects, artists, workmen, and civic planners, a dinner was given in the Madison Square Hall for Daniel H. Burnham by the New York men who had worked with him.[8] The *Tribune*, the next day, devoted three columns to the "testimonial dinner" in which the names of the guests, the decoration of the hall, and the speeches themselves were duly reported.[9] Howells sat at the head table, with Charles Eliot Norton, Charles Dudley Warner, and many other friends. Through the masses of red roses heaped on the white damask, he could look down at the guests before him—his brothers-in-law, William Rutherford Mead and Larkin Mead; Frederick Law Olmsted, landscape architect of the Exposition; Richard Watson Gilder, editor of *The Century*; John La Farge and Augustus Saint-Gaudens, painters and sculptors; Brander Matthews, critic and novelist—to mention only a few of those who had gathered to celebrate the completion of their united efforts.

As the orchestra behind the palms subsided, the guest of honor, Daniel Burnham, arose to say that the real glory of the occasion belonged to the architects, artists, and builders, who "have vied with each other for a common

result which, as individuals, they have subordinated themselves to bring about; in short, they have been what all
Americans should be in public matters—unselfish. (Applause.)" Richard Watson Gilder then offered a toast "To
the White City":

Say not, "Greece is no more!"
Through the clear morn
On light winds borne
Her white-winged soul sinks on the New World's breast.
Ah, happy West—
Greece flowers anew, and all her temples soar! [10]

Charles Dudley Warner drank to "Columbus," and
Charles Eliot Norton lifted his glass to "The Arts." Other
speeches followed, and each was greeted by a round of
applause from the "ladies in the balcony," as well as from
the gentlemen on the floor. Letters and telegrams from
President Cleveland, from several governors, from well-
wishers abroad were read aloud to the assembly and the
"brilliant dinner" was ended—a fitting prelude to the opening of the Fair a little over a month later.[11]

Howells charteristically offered no toast on this occasion and made no speech; instead, he thoughtfully enjoyed
the genial atmosphere of the celebration at which his two
brothers-in-law and many of his friends, both artists and
writers, were present.[12] Perhaps his mind was still occupied
with Mr. Twelvemough's account of the Altrurian Traveler in New Hampshire. When the Fair was dedicated in
the autumn of 1892, Howells had been collecting his
thoughts on the relation of Christian Socialism to the problems of modern society that were to find expression in the
first series of Altrurian essays, recounted by the writer of
society novels. Howells was still concerned with the Altrurian's criticisms of this country at the time of the Burn-

ham dinner; nor had he completed the series, when, on May 1, 1893, Cleveland threw the switch that illuminated the Fair with thousands of "electrics" at the grand opening of the most elaborate World Exposition so far ever attempted.[13]

Several weeks after these events, Howells received a letter from his friend Hamlin Garland, who had spent a few days at the Fair, asking whether he planned to take part in a Literary Congress to be held on the grounds in July. Howells replied firmly that he had no such intention. "If the authors assembled need guidance," he added, "*you* are the leader for them." [14] Howells was impelled, however, to journey out to the Fair in September, not so much because of the urging of Garland and other friends, as because John Brisben Walker himself visited the Exposition on July 4, 1893,[15] and returned to New York full of fresh enthusiasm. Though *The Cosmopolitan* since the beginning of his editorship had been reflecting the progress of the Fair,[16] Walker's experience at the scene moved him to turn the entire September issue to an account of the White City and its implications for the future. On July 4, 1893, Walker reported in his introductory essay, more than 350,000 people were in attendance in spite of sweltering summer weather. Indeed, he added,

the very brain of the world may be said to have been concentrated in the lecture halls of this University of Democracy.

"The World's College of Democracy" [17] is the title Walker chose for his essay, as well as the name he gave the Fair. No doubt, on his return to New York, Walker suggested to Howells, whose Altrurian series would end in the October issue of *The Cosmopolitan*,[18] that he should make a hurried trip to the scene and weave his thoughts into a

fresh series of Altrurian essays. "The Letters of an Altrurian Traveller" began with the November, 1893, issue
of the magazine; by December the Altrurian was viewing
a realization of his dreams for America in the Grecian
buildings on the shores of Lake Michigan.

Like all successful world's fairs, the Chicago Exposition
called forth exclamations of wonder, scorn and prophesy,
characteristic of the gazer. Walker, for example, as he
strolled over the grounds, thought he saw in the gleaming
white buildings exhibiting the products of seventy-five na-
tions a tangible evidence of progress. "It is safe to esti-
mate," he wrote, "that our civilization and advance in the
liberal arts will be moved forward by a quarter of a century as a result of this marvellous Exposition." Nor was
this defender of the common man thinking only of ma-
chinery and architecture; he also gloried in the impact of
these achievements on the people. Glancing about at the
Fourth of July crowds, he exclaimed,

> What a collection of people amidst what magnificent sur-
> roundings! . . . every bounty of nature, every magnificence
> of architecture, every creation of art, is brought together and
> opened for the benefit, not of the rich, not of the great, not
> of genius, not of the fortunate class, not of the few but of all,
> including the humblest citizen. Nor did the wisdom which has
> brought together these many people from every part of our
> vast nation intend this fairy land of democracy simply as a
> means of pleasure.

No doubt a reasonable proportion of the 350,000 citizens
who roamed the Fair on July 4, 1893, found their own
"means of pleasure"; to Walker, however, the Exposition
was "a school in which the millions are entered for a course
of instruction." [19]

Two more sophisticated visitors, Charles Eliot Norton

and Henry Adams, arrived at the gates of the Fair—as did Howells—a month before they closed. The elderly Norton, still lecturing on the history of art to crowded classes at Harvard, enjoyed his exhausting visit to the Exposition, for he regarded the Fair as a "promise of the future." He wrote to a friend on his return to the East that he would like to live permanently "where there is so strong and wholesome a communal feeling." Not only did Norton, strolling about the vast area, admire the landscaping, executed by his friend and associate, Frederick Law Olmsted—the classical buildings, the electric fountains, the gondolas, and the canals; he liked, above all, the Chicagoans themselves. "I have never seen Americans from whom one could draw happier auguries for the future of America, than some of the men I saw at Chicago," he wrote. In short,

The Fair, in spite of its amazing incongruities, and its immense "border" of vulgarities, was on the whole a great promise, even a great pledge. It, at least, forbids despair.[20]

Henry Adams, who visited the grounds for the second time in September, asked the question as to "whether the American people knew where they were driving"; as usual he found ample room for despair in the fact that the Fair provided no answer. As he stood before the dynamo in the Hall of Engineering, he decided that here, undoubtedly, was power, but power without direction. But "the Exposition itself defied philosophy." One might seek in vain for "explanations," one might find fault "till the last gate closed," still, concluded Adams, "as a scenic display, Paris had never approached it." Beauty was, indeed, achieved; however, "since Noah's Ark, no such Babel of loose and ill-joined, such vague and ill-defined and unrelated thoughts and half-thoughts and experimental outcries as the Exposition, had ever ruffled the surface of the Lakes." [21]

If the "lesson" contributed by the Fair to the education of Henry Adams was equivocal—as were all of the lessons taught him in the course of his lifelong education—the ideas carried away by Hamlin Garland after a summer in Chicago were simple and clear—old "idols" were "crumbling"; welcome "the new." Garland read before the Literary Congress in July a paper on "Local Color in the Novel" defending the realists—or, to use his term, the "veritists." His attack on the established romantic novelists caused a literary argument in newspapers and magazines which lasted through the autumn.[22] Indeed, Eugene Field, in his daily column in the *Chicago Record*, suggested that Howells' visit to Chicago in September was for the purpose of rescuing his younger friend from the furor he had created.[23] Studying the impressionistic paintings from France and Spain hung among the old masters in the Art Building, Garland extended his understanding of the modern movement and interpreted it in a lecture on "Local Color in Art." These addresses, and several others pointing in the same direction, were collected the following year in a small volume, appropriately named *Crumbling Idols.* Garland saw in the Exposition a cultural hope for the whole country. Out of the vast wealth of the West, a new national art was emerging:

Already Chicago claims to have pushed New York from her seat as ruler of our commerce. . . . The rise of Chicago as a literary and art centre is a question only of time, and of a very short time; for the Columbian Exposition has taught her her own capabilities in something higher than business.

Garland realized that "there are scores of original young writers and artists just rising to power in the West," [24] with whom he wished to associate. Just as Howells had recently moved from Boston to the newer literary center, New York, so Garland, his younger disciple, transferred his home at this time to what he thought would be the future cultural center of the country, Chicago.

Howells' five-day visit to the Fair a month before its closing in no way changed his life; it did, however, supply him with an example of "pure Altruria." In the December, 1893, issue of *The Cosmopolitan*, Howells, through the Altrurian, poured out his account of the White City.[25] This glimpse of the Fair, built by thousands of hands to last for a few months only, showed Homos for the first time the hope latent in democracy. "The Fair City is a bit of Altruria," he wrote to Cyril:

it is as if the capital of one of our Regions had set sail and landed somewhere on the shores of the vast inland sea, where the Fair City lifts its domes and columns.

Here, in "their pitiless economic struggle," the Americans had lent themselves to the work of building an ideally beautiful city, with no thought of money returns. The capitalists, unwillingly at first, had put themselves in the hands of the artists; together they had produced "the greatest marvel of the competitive world," which, in the end, proved profitable in money returns as well. Aristides particularly applauded the Director for having relinquished the notion of a competition among artists, in favor of "the free coöperation of the arts through the foremost artists of the country." Individual artists from various areas were chosen to execute different buildings, "and for the first time since the great ages, since the beauty of antiquity and

the elegance of the renaissance, the arts were reunited."
Here, in building the Fair City, gifted minds and sensitive
spirits worked "for the pleasure of it, the pride of it, the
pure good of it." The very thought moved the Altrurian,
he said, to actual tears, causing the pillared porches to swim
before his vision. We can do no better than to take "an
electric launch" with the Altrurian and share his vision of
the Fair:

I first saw the Fair City by night, from one of the electric
launches which ply upon the lagoon; and under the dimmed
heaven, in the splendor of the hundred moony arc-lamps of
the esplanades, and the myriad incandescent bubbles that
beaded the white quays, and defined the structural lines of
dome and porch and pediment, I found myself in the midst
of the Court of Honor. . . . We fronted the beautiful Agricultural building, which I think fitly the finest in the city.

The Agricultural Building, to which both Rutherford
and Larkin Mead had contributed, called forth special
ejaculations. Since Howells' friend, Augustus Saint-
Gaudens, was Director of the Sculpture of the Exposition,
we are willing to allow the Altrurian an extra glance at the
statues as we glide through the enchanted air:

On our right was the Administrative building with its coro-
neted dome, and the magnificent sculptured fountain before
it, turned silver in the radiance of the clustered electric jets at
either side. On our right was the glorious peristyle, serene,
pure, silent, lifting a population of statues against the night,
and dividing the lagoon from the lake, whose soft moan came
appealingly through the pillared spaces, and added a divine
heartache to my ecstacy [sic]. Here a group of statuary
showed itself prominently on quay or cornice; we caught the
flamy curve of a bridge's arch; a pale column lifted its jutting
prores into the light; but nothing insisted; all was harmonized
to one effect of beauty, as if in symbol of the concentrated

impulses which had created it. For the moment I could not believe that so foul a thing as money could have been even the means of its creation.

Though Mr. Homos scorned money, he was emphatically a practical man with an interest in the policing of the Dream City, in the cleanup squads, in the drainage of the swamps on which the dream was built, and in the villages of Indians, Chinese, Africans, and Turks erected on the Plaisance. Here, among the shops and cafés, the Altrurian hoped "to get upon speaking terms with these average people," for whom presumably all this beauty was created. But "the vast bulk, the massed members of that immense equality" of our democracy, which filled the streets and waterways of the Fair, remained reserved and unapproachable as far as Mr. Homos was concerned. In America, the Altrurian wrote his friend, silent people were docilely content to eat their lunches out of boxes while the rich flocked to restaurants. "Everywhere the economic inequality is as passively accepted as if it were a natural inequality, like difference in height or strength." Several weeks before Howells' visit to the Fair, his friend, Thomas Sergeant Perry, had made a similar observation about "the great, gentle, pathetic, kindly American people" at the Exposition. "One never sees," he wrote in the *Boston Evening Transcript* of September 8, 1893, "any rudeness or selfish indifference to others' comfort. It is the most orderly and decent crowd that the world has ever seen, as well as the most silent."

Mr. Homos, strolling through this well-mannered crowd, soon encountered Mr. Bullion, the banker he had known the previous summer. They enjoyed a bottle of Rhenish wine together in "the gravelled court of Old Vienna," and talked of the effect the Fair must have on American civilization. Mr. Bullion hoped that the classical architecture might "sober and refine the artists" who build houses for the people. The Altrurian tried to make him understand that the "simplicity of Greek architecture came out of the simplicity of Greek life, and the preference given in the Greek state to the intellectual over the industrial, to art over business."

I pointed out that until there was some enlightened municipal or national control of the matter, no excellence of example could avail, but that the classicism of the Fair City would become, among a wilful and undisciplined people, a fad with the rich and a folly with the poor, and not a real taste with either class. . . . I ventured so far as to say that the whole competitive world, with the exception of a few artists, had indeed lost the sense of beauty, and I even added that the Americans as a people seemed never to have had it at all.

Entranced as the Altrurian was by the Dream City, he knew that it was only made of plaster, that the Grecian fronts were false; that the people who wandered from pavilion to pavilion had no feeling other than wonder at the vast fairyland to which they had journeyed from desolate farms and chaotic cities. "I do not believe this example will have any lasting effect with you unless you become Altrurianized," Mr. Homos said to the banker as they parted.

On October 25, 1893, a month after his return to New York, Howells wrote to Norton,[26] commented on their recent encounter at the Fair, and told him to watch for the December issue of *The Cosmopolitan* for his view of the Exposition. Howells had already completed his essay for the December issue of the magazine and had turned his attention—or that of the Altrurian—to absorbing "the shock of American conditions" as he experienced them in

New York. What Aristides thought of Babylon (New York) is contained in the nine communications, beginning in January, 1894, and ending the following September, which make up the remaining "Letters From an Altrurian Traveller" to his friend.

Aristides' reference to New York as Babylon suggests that to Howells the White City was the New Jerusalem, the City of God. The story of the Children of Israel repining in captivity in Babylon, waiting to be led back to the New Jerusalem, was familiar enough to Howells, of course, and had been since he had listened as a boy to his Swedenborgian father read aloud from *The New Jerusalem*. Howells knew the story, too, from Goldsmith's retelling of the tale in his poem, *The Captivity*.[27] These overtones were in his mind as he gazed on the serene beauty of the White City and thought of the ugliness and confusion of his Babylon. Howells wrote to the artist, Howard Pyle—also a Swedenborgian—soon after his return to New York, that he was engaged in a "second series" of Altrurian essays. Howells then remarked:

At Chicago, Burnham, the Director of Works, at the Fair, who is of Swedenborgian training, told me that when he told his mother of the magnificent consensus of will and aims in the capitalists and artists who created its beauty, she saw in it a vision of the New Jerusalem, and a direct leading of the Lord toward "the wonder that shall be," when men all work in harmony, and not in rivalry.[28]

Howells' friends among the Christian Socialists were also fond of referring to the concept of a return to "The City of God"; St. Augustine's phrase was used as the title of a poem in the May, 1890, issue of *The Dawn*.[29] At the head of the page Zachariah is quoted:

Jerusalem shall be called a city of God. . . . There shall yet old men and women dwell in the streets of Jerusalem, and every man with his staff in his hand for every age. And the streets of the city shall be full of boys and girls playing in the streets thereof.

In the next issue of *The Dawn*,[30] Christianity is referred to "as a ladder for climbing up to the New Jerusalem . . . the best, the safest, the strongest, and purest the world has ever seen."

The term, the New Jerusalem, had been applied to the Fair, soon after its opening. An essay for *Harper's*, printed at that time, came to a close with this triumphant thought:

Perhaps some freed spiritual intelligence who had had experience in the building of the New Jerusalem became conscious of a possible improvement, and longing to verify it, came down for a brief period to join the band of builders and distinguish his share of work in the Dream City. To see this miracle of harmonious form at sunset, with all its lovely length shining down the lagoon, is easily to believe in its heavenly origin.[31]

A writer for the July, 1893, issue of *Scribner's Magazine* predicted that

"The Heavenly City," the "New Jerusalem" with gates of gold and pearl, which in one questionable shape or another hovers in the hopeful, faithful fancy of so many sons of Adam, will here find a realization, supplanting or exalting the ideal which has hitherto not always been to the glory of Heaven.[32]

Thus informed by newspapers and magazines as to what they might expect to experience at the Columbian Exposition, the harmonious classical architecture of the White City on the shores of Lake Michigan, illuminated nightly by 150,000 incandescent lamps, seemed to the thousands of visitors who drifted through it a marvelous realization of the New Jerusalem. Here, undoubtedly, the common man —when not munching his sandwiches on the Plaisance or wasting his money in the shooting galleries—was unconsciously absorbing the beauty, majesty, and promise of two great traditions, the classical and the Christian. Merchants, bankers, artists, architects—all had worked together that the farm hand from Iowa might come into his rightful inheritance in the great new promise of democracy. So, indeed, did Homos-Howells interpret the message of the Exposition—as did many other visitors to the Fair. Neither Howells, nor any of the many notable admirers of this New Jerusalem of 1893, commented on the fact that Friedrich A. Krupp, builder of the "Cannon King," [33] had sent from Germany an elaborate display of guns and armaments, far more menacing than any weapons known to the veterans of the Civil War who visited the exhibit, nor that one of the most popular displays at the Fair was a sham battleship, the U.S.S. *Illinois*, lying at anchor in Lake Michigan.

Some years later, after he had witnessed the un-Altrurian activities of this country during the Spanish-American War in 1898, Howells took up once more the tale of Aristides Homos, this time allowing him to remain in his own country. In the Introduction to these later adventures, entitled *Through the Eye of the Needle* (1907), Howells summarized, without comment, Aristides' visit to the Fair, observing merely that "in the early autumn of 1893, he spent several days at the great Columbian Exposition in Chicago." He made no reference at this later date to the glorious dream of universal brotherhood which Aristides (and Howells) enjoyed in 1893.

NOTES

1. *The Cosmopolitan*, XVI (November, 1893), 110. *Letters*, p. 13.
2. *Idem.*, December, 1893, 218. *Letters*, p. 20. These first two letters in the series were not reprinted by Howells after their original appearance in *The Cosmopolitan*. See Notes to Introduction of this book.
3. *Idem.*, XVII (January, 1894), 259–260. *Letters*, pp. 35–36. This Letter was reprinted, with important alterations, in *Impressions and Experiences*, 1896. The title of the essay was then changed from "A Bit of Altruria in New York" to "Glimpses of Central Park." The next two letters, February and March, 1894, "Aspects and Impressions of a Plutocratic City" and "Plutocratic Contrasts and Contradictions" were combined in *Impressions and Experiences* under the title, "New York Streets." The remaining six essays were republished as Part I of *Through the Eye of the Needle*, 1907. At this time Part II was added and an Introduction written to the whole volume. The twelve essays on "A Traveller From Altruria" (*The Cosmopolitan*, XIV–XV, November, 1892–October, 1893) appeared as a book *A Traveler From Altruria* in May, 1894.
4. The *New York Herald*, Sunday (September 23, 1894), Sixth Section, p. 7. Unsigned article, accompanied by pictures of Swinburne, Wilde, Morris, Shaw, Bellamy, and Howells. The *New York Daily Tribune*, Sunday, September 30, 1894, p. 14.
5. Francis Davis Millet (1846–1912), painter, author, war correspondent, and illustrator, became Master of Ceremonies at the Exposition.
6. "The Decoration of the Exposition," *Scribner*, XII (September, 1892), 693–707. "The Designers of the Fair," *Harper's*, LXXXV (November, 1892), 873–883.
7. The Transportation Building, designed by Louis Henry Sullivan, was the only building to break the monotony of white stucco Grecian. For a contemporary comment on the bad taste of this departure, see "The Department of Transporta-

tion," *The World's Fair, Pictorial History of the Columbian Exposition*, XXIV (1893), pp. 414-415.

8. See "Our Exposition at Chicago," by Julian Ralph. *Harper's*, LXXXIV (January, 1892), 205-214.

9. The *New York Tribune*, Sunday (March 26, 1893), pp. 1-2.

10. "The White City," by Richard Watson Gilder. *Century*, XLVI (February, 1893), 22.

11. The World's Columbian Exposition was dedicated on October 21, 1892. It opened on May 1, 1893, and closed the following October 30. For a description of these events, see *The World's Fair* as cited in Note 7.

12. William Rutherford Mead, of the firm of McKim, Mead & White, which designed the Agricultural Building. Larkin Mead designed the pediment of the building, the "Triumph of Ceres." Augustus Saint-Gaudens sculptured the figure of Diana on the dome of the building. La Farge, Chase, Cox, Alma-Tadema, and many other artists known to Howells, contributed to the Fair. On a panel in the Woman's Building Howells' daughter Mildred was painted by her friend, Lucia Fairchild.

13. An art critic of London commented, "The Columbian Exposition of 1893, as it excels all former 'World Fairs' in extent, also presents many novel, characteristic and attractive features." ("Chicago and the Columbian Fair," *The Art Journal*, XLX, 1893.) Between the Crystal Palace Exposition of 1851 and the Columbian Exposition, five World's Fairs had been held—three in Paris (1867, 1878 and 1889), one in Vienna (1873), and one in Philadelphia, the Centennial of 1876.

14. Letter to Hamlin Garland, May 28, 1893. Library of the University of Southern California. See Donald Pizer, "A Summer Campaign in Chicago: Hamlin Garland Defends a Native Art." *Western Humanities Review* (Autumn, 1959), pp. 375-382.

15. For a description of "American Day at the Fair," July 4, 1893, see "The World Fair," *The Cosmopolitan*, XV (September, 1893), 794-816.

16. As soon as Walker took over *The Cosmopolitan* he published an article by Charles B. Farwell, United States Senator, followed by another by William Waldorf Astor, the first urging Chicago's candidacy for the Fair and the second New York's. (*The Cosmopolitan*, VIII, November and December, 1889.) When the question was settled, Walker continued to publish articles about the Fair by such writers as Paul Bourget, Walter

Besant, F. Hopkinson Smith, Franz Boas, and Julian Hawthorne.

17. *The Cosmopolitan*, XV (September, 1893), 524. In the same issue, Walker wrote a second article, "Transportation, Old and New," in which he observed that "the electric railway which traverses the length of the Exposition grounds, is one of the greatest delights of the entire Exposition," p. 587.

18. *The Coast of Bohemia*, discussed in Chapter IV of this volume, was also completed in October, 1893. It is interesting to notice that Howells in this slight novel, which caused him so much trouble, also described a Fair, in this case the Pymantoning County Fair, of Pymantoning County, Ohio. The name "Pymantoning" is Howells' alteration of Pymatuning, a town in Northeastern Ohio.

19. Walker, *op. cit.*, pp. 517–520.

20. To Henry B. Fuller, October 13, 1893. *The Letters of Charles Eliot Norton*, II (1913), 218.

21. *The Education of Henry Adams* (1918), p. 339.

22. See Lucy Monroe, "Chicago Letter," The *Critic* (July 22, 1893), p. 60. Cited by Pizer, *op. cit.*

23. "Sharps and Flats," The *Chicago Record*, September 28, 1893, p. 4. Cited by Pizer, *op. cit.*

24. *Crumbling Idols, Twelve Essays on Art and Literature*, by Hamlin Garland, Introduction by Robert E. Spiller, 1952. Pp. 152–153.

25. XVI, 218–232.

26. Manuscript letter. Houghton Library, Harvard.

27. Goldsmith, *op. cit.*, pp. 46–47. *Psalms*, CXXX, 8.

28. *Life in Letters*, II, 40.

29. By James Yeams, *The Dawn*, May, 1890, pp. 26–27. Zachariah, VIII, 3–5.

30. "To-day's Necessity," by John Brown. *The Dawn*, June, 1890, p. 72.

31. "A Dream City," by Candace Wheeler, *Harper's*, LXXXVI (May, 1893), 836.

32. "Foreground and Vista at the Fair," by W. H. Gibson. *Scribner's*, XIV (July, 1893), 29.

33. See a poem, "Coast Gun I, 33. Krupp Pavilion," by Martha Foote Crow, which begins, with an address to the gun itself: "Thy lips, stern argument is more for peace/Than War, O Cannon-King." *The Cosmopolitan*, XVI (December, 1893), 157.

Chapter VI

The Traveler's Return
New York, 1893–1894

"Well, my dear Cyril, I have returned to this Babylon, you see, from my fortnight's stay in that vision of Altruria at the great Fair in Chicago," wrote Aristides to his friend on October 24, 1893. Having seen with his own eyes "what might be, in the Fair City," the Altrurian returned to "what the Americans say must be, in New York," and shrank, as he did on his first arrival in this country, from the physical as well as the moral ugliness of that vast American city.

Having been "hurled precariously" over the "continental spaces" between Chicago and New York in a sleeping car that might have been "designed for the state progress of some barbarous prince through his dominions," the Altrurian drove to a hotel overlooking Central Park—the old Plaza, on the corner of Fifty-ninth Street and Fifth Avenue. Though his hotel was itself "one of the most preposterous of the structures which disfigure the city," his window allowed him to look into "the leafy depths" of the "vast forest" of the Park, and to forget for a moment the ugliness of "the great unwieldy monster" lying about him. "The bruise" of the Altrurian's "encounter with the brute ugliness of this place" was twofold: the buildings themselves, constructed "with savage disregard to one another," were a physical offense; they were also a source of moral suffering since they offered "incomparable animal comfort" on a princely scale to a few and abject poverty to many. The best thing about the Altrurian's hotel was that it was a sort of gateway to the Park. The visitor was able to descend to the street level when he wished and to lose himself in the woods of Central Park, "as sweet and friendly as our groves at home." Here the Traveler liked to wander, "unmolested by the crowds that make them their resort so harmlessly that even the sylvan life there is unafraid."

It was, of course, pure self-indulgence, the Altrurian admitted, that had led him to take a room in an expensive hotel overlooking Central Park. But, he pointed out to his friend,

> You must remember the perpetual homesickness gnawing at my heart, and you must realize how doubly strange an Altrurian finds himself in any country of the plutocratic world; and then, I think, you will understand why I spend, and even waste, so much of my time lingering in this lovely place.[1]

In September, 1896, when Howells reprinted portions of this letter and the two which followed it,[2] in *Impressions and Experiences*, the Altrurian's comments on New York became Howells' own—as, indeed, the reader might have suspected, from the beginning, they were. Though Aristides Homos was, at the opening of the Altrurian essays, in danger of being merely an "idea," while the very human Mr. Twelvemough was plainly a "reality," even before the two had left New Hampshire, Mr. Homos had become more "real" than his shadowy host. Now, in re-editing the letters of the Altrurian to form a contribution to an attractive volume of "timely" essays on the general subject of life in

New York, Howells avowedly became the spokesman. Borrowing Mr. Homos' own words, Howells addressed his "impressions and experiences" directly to New Yorkers who were then more interested in the changing ways and customs of their rapidly growing metropolis than in the darker aspects of social problems. All references to the Traveler were omitted, and Howells spoke in the first person, thus tacitly admitting that he himself had been the Traveler from Altruria since his first appearance in the New Hampshire hotel.[3]

Not only was Howells an older, wearier man when he undertook the re-editing of several of Aristides' letters to include in his new volume of essays, but he was also addressing himself to a more sophisticated circle of readers, related, perhaps, to those whom Howells had gently satirized when he had met them several years earlier on the verandah of the New England hotel. Therefore, the first five pages of Aristides' letter (paraphrased above) were simply omitted, as being far too sharply critical of New York for New Yorkers to enjoy. Gone were the references to "the poor negroes who make up the beds in the sleepers" on the trains between Chicago and New York; to the silver-plated spitoons which accompany "the filthy national habit of spitting"; to "the fleeced and imperilled passengers," who, neither "mangled nor massacred," arrive at their destination "from two to six hours late." No longer was the reader asked "to consider whether a public management of public affairs is not as well in economics as in politics." Instead, Howells began his essay, now called "Glimpses of Central Park," [4] with the following mild sentence taken directly from the fifth page of Aristides' letter to Cyril:

This morning, as I sat on a bench in one of the most frequented walks of Central Park, I could almost have touched the sparrows on the sprays about me; a squirrel, foraging for nuts, climbed on my knees, as if to explore my pockets.

But, we must remind ourselves, it was Howells, and not Aristides, who was sitting on the bench in the pleasant October air. The essential thought of both observers was the same: "the security and immunity of the Park" offered the hint Americans were beginning to accept; what is the common property of all is also in "the personal charge of every one in the community." Howells, like the Altrurian, regarded with sympathy "the sodden tramps," looking like "forlorn wild beasts"; the poor woman, with "a paper bundle on the seat beside her." Howells, too, lamented the vulgar display of overdressed ladies riding in their open broughams with lackies perched on the seat behind them; nor did he approve of the aping of European manners by the throngs of strollers in the Park. Nothing new was added to the Altrurian's letter when Howells converted it into an essay; however, many of the more downright statements were deleted. For example, Howells omitted Aristides' concluding thought, expressed to Cyril, that,

without economic equality there can be no social equality, and, finally, there can be no political equality; for money corrupts the franchise, the legislature and the judiciary here, just as it used to do with us in the old days before the Evolution. Of all the American fatuities, none seems to me more deplorable than the pretension that with their conditions it can ever be otherwise, or that simple manhood can assert itself successfully in the face of such power as money wields over the very soul of man. At best, the common man can only break from time to time, into insolent defiance, pending his chance to make himself an uncommon man with money.[5]

To both Howells and Aristides, "the lesson" of Central Park was that when it is used "in the spirit of fraternity and equality," those who enjoy it have glimpsed a beauty which they might make perpetual in their lives; when however, it was "invaded by the plutocratic motives of the strife that raves all round it in the city outside," its benefits were marred by contempt and envy. It was clear that "ninety-nine Americans out of every hundred" would, if they could, "flaunt their luxury in the face of poverty." Aristides—but not Howells—added:

They would not feel, as we should, the essential immorality of its deformity; they would not perceive that its ludicrous disproportion was the outward expression of an inward ugliness.

The great trouble about living in New York, both to Aristides and to Howells, was that "you cannot anywhere get away from the misery of life," always to be found, said Aristides, "in those unhappy countries where there are rich and poor"—a phrase not repeated by Howells when he reprinted the letter. One might think that the rich themselves would have objected to "the mere loathliness of poverty" and wished to rid themselves of the sight. They were, however, wrote Aristides, "the slaves of habit" and were hardly aware of the "vital reality" of their surroundings.

It is only a luckless exile from Altruria like myself who sees them in their dreadful verity, and has a living sense of them; and I, too, lose this at times.

The Altrurian, then, furnished Howells with the fresh eyes of the exile returning to the city. Howells, however, when speaking later in his own person, toned down the comments of the Altrurian. Both men tended to lose their sharpness of perception after they were lulled to sleep by the comforts of hotels, the fascination of streets and parks, and, above all, by the disarming kindness and hospitality of Americans. Howells perpetuated this more complacent state of mind in *Impressions and Experiences* by deleting the first violent reactions of the Altrurian when he found himself again in Babylon, and assembling chiefly the milder views characteristic of an older writer. Howells had become "the observer" rather than "the stranger" and could no longer look with such a direct gaze at "the terrible continuity of conditions in the world outside of Altruria." Aristides was thinking of his homeland to which he would return; for Howells, Altruria existed only in his own heart. Howells could not take "the next train to Chicago," still less "the next steamer to Altruria"; he could, however, keep clearly in mind his concept of an ideal America, though the hope of its achievement seemed less bright as he grew older and more disillusioned.

Letters IV and V of *The Cosmopolitan* series [6] became "New York Streets," the last essay of *Impressions and Experiences*. But these letters, collected only two years after their original appearance, were re-edited for *Harper's* by Howells, who, though he no longer spoke from the "Study" of *Harper's Monthly* and had not yet assumed the editorship of the "Easy Chair," was, nevertheless, working in close co-operation with the Harper organization. One is not surprised to find whole paragraphs deleted from Aristides' letters—paragraphs reflecting Howells' basic social thought, which Walker had encouraged. Aristides, for example, had written:

> Every city of the plutocratic world must be an outrage to Altrurian senses, as you already understand, but I doubt if I could ever make you understand the abominable condition of the New York streets during the snowy months of the past winter, when for weeks no attempt was made to

remove their accumulated filth. At their best, they would be intolerable to us; at their worst, they are inconceivable and wholly indescribable. The senses witness their condition, but the mind refuses to receive the evidence of the senses; and nothing can be more pathetic, more comic, than the resolution of the New Yorkers in ignoring it. (*Letter IV*)

These accusing words Howells did not include in his later essay. Just as the Altrurian had glimpsed in the Chicago Exposition a hope for the America of the future, so, in his walks through Central Park, Mr. Homos had found "a bit of Altruria" in New York. Homos had written to Cyril that he loved to linger near the Park—which, like the Fair, was laid out by Olmsted—"because it affords a hope for New York that I feel so distinctly nowhere else in New York." The "experimental nature" of the metropolis, to be sure, sometimes suggested "that it may be the first city of America to Altrurianize." But would New Yorkers ever understand that this could be "lastingly done only through a change of the economic conditions"? Only in Central Park did these ruthless crowds seem to become nature-loving Altrurians and "brotherly" in their relations to one another. Since New Yorkers, like Altrurians, loved to stroll in Central Park, Howells, in re-editing this letter, merely toned down some of the Traveler's moralizing and renamed the essay "Glimpses of Central Park."

Howells himself, who lived for years near "the gate of Central Park," a few steps west of the Altrurian's hotel, enjoyed walking through its shaded alleys and curving paths. Like his more outspoken prototype, he frequently plunged into the traffic of the wide north-and-south avenues and thence into the narrower, meaner cross streets, always returning to Central Park as a touchstone of what might be achieved if the civic imagination of the New

Yorker could be inspired. As Homos expressed the thought to Cyril,

The Park, which is the physical heart of New York, is Altrurian already. In the contrasts of rich and poor, which you can no more escape there then you can in the city streets, you are, indeed, afflicted with that sense of absurdity, of impossibility, so comforting to the American when he strives to imagine Altrurian conditions, and gets no farther than to imagine the creatures of a plutocratic civilization in them. He imagines that, in an Altrurian state, people must have the same motives, interests, anxieties, which he has always known them to have, and which they carry with them into Central Park, and only lay aside for a moment in response to the higher appeal which its equal opportunities make. But then, at moments these care-worn, greed-worn souls do put off the burden of their inequality, their superiority or their inferiority, and meet on the same broad level of humanity; and I wish, my dear Cyril, that you would always keep its one great oasis in your thoughts, as you follow me in my wanderings through this vast commercial desert. It is the token, if not the pledge, of happier things, and, while I remain here, it will be always to me a precious image of home. (*Letter IV*, p. 417.)

This "precious image" of Altruria, neatly omitted from Howells' later essay, clearly remained in Homos' mind as he traversed Fifth Avenue, observed how relentlessly business and poverty were "everywhere slowly or swiftly eating their way into the haunts of respectability," plunged into the areas "abandoned to the poverty which festers in the squalid houses and swarms day and night in the squalid streets."

The tenement houses of New York, the foundries, the dingy wharves, the breweries, the unrelieved ugliness of dirty streets—all this sent the Altrurian back to his hotel "heart-sick," realizing, as he did, that "in the plutocratic conditions," poverty and confusion were incurable. They must always exist "till time shall be no more," said Americans to their visitor, "with an unconscious blasphemy of the ever-enduring Good, and, unless the conditions change, I must confess that they have reason for their faith in evil." This inner strife in Howells' mind never appeared in his essay for *Harper's*, for he drew his pencil through such observations as those in the following lines of Aristides' letter:

You must lose the thought of what is below the surface everywhere and in everything in America, if you would possess your soul from the pain perpetually threatening it; and I am afraid, my dear Cyril, that if you could be suddenly transported to my side, and behold what underlies all life here, with your fresh Altrurian eyes, you would not be more shocked at the sight than at me, who, knowing it all, can ever have a moment's peace in my knowledge. (*Letter IV*)

Your very rest at night, said Homos, depended upon your ability to ignore "a thousand facts, which, if you recognize them, turn and rend you, and instill their poison into your lacerated soul." The "fortunate children" of a plutocracy knew, in the bottom of their hearts, that only by "mere chance" [7] they were not among the abased and the destitute; if they were ever led by their sympathies to an act of charity, they soon learned that "charity itself corrupts and debases, and that finally it is no remedy." After experiencing the "anguish of impotency," most Americans took "refuge from themselves in a wilful ignorance, sometimes lastingly, sometimes transiently, of the things in their life that disturb and displease them."

Aristides' account of the state of mind of Americans in the face of wrong which disturbed them was a reflection of Howells' own distress in the face of social injustice;

like most Americans, he wrote, "I have learned to shut my eyes to it." Since one was powerless to act, "the wrong must be a sort of right," he concluded wearily. This "infernal juggle of the mind" made the Traveler doubt his own reality, the reality of his former happiness, and, indeed, the very existence of Altruria. Since Altruria was to Howells a symbol of his dream of America at that time, it was clear that the dream itself was in danger of fading, as he reflected upon "the conditions" prevailing in New York. The last paragraph of Homos' letter, which was not reprinted in *Impressions and Experiences*, reflected Howells' inner doubts and fears for his country. "I beseech you," Aristides begged Cyril,

write me as often as you can, and as fully and vividly. Tell me of our country, remind me of the state where men dwell together as brothers; use every device to make it living and real to me; for here I often lose the memory and the sense of it, and at all times I have a weakened sense of the justice and mercy that I once thought ruled this world, but which the Americans think rules only the world to come. (*Letter IV*)

Unfortunately, no cheering letter from Cyril arrived to break into Aristides' mood as he walked the New York streets which led from "nowhere to nowhere." Instead there was Letter V, November 15, 1893, from Homos to his friend, called in *The Cosmopolitan* of March, 1894, "Plutocratic Contrasts and Contradictions." Portions of this letter formed the second half of the essay, "New York Streets," in *Impressions and Experiences*; as in the case of Letter IV, the more hopeless, the more troubled paragraphs were removed.[8] For the Traveler from an imaginary land could speak out more frankly in *The Cosmopolitan* of 1894, under Walker's liberal editorship, than could Howells when he was recasting his two letters to form one essay in a Harper publication.

Since the hotel chosen by the Traveler was near the apartment to which Howells had moved in 1892,[9] the words the Altrurian found to describe the buildings of New York were exactly suited to Howells' use, for he considered his apartment house, as well as the Altrurian's hotel, a part of the architectural disorder which added to the confusion of a city perpetually in transition. He described his own abode as rising six or seven stories higher than a neighboring building and terminating in a sort of mansard, topping a romanesque cliff of yellow brick and red sandstone, which had no known architectural term proper to it. The "civic disorder of what succeeds" was probably a very good description of West Fifty-ninth Street as it appeared to Howells in the first half of the 1890's. "From the summit of this enormous acclivity there is a precipitous fall of twelve stories to the roof of the next edifice," which was a grocery store, by the side of which was, first a florist shop, and then a photographer's studio. After a further descent of three stories, one reached "a drinking-saloon, one story in height, with a brick front and a wooden side." This "delirium of line and colors," this "savage anarchy of shapes," should have been rendered perceptible to the dull American sense, says Homos, by "the general experience of the beauty of the Fair City of Chicago." But, as Aristides pointed out, what actually existed was

the necessary and inexorable effect of that uncivic individuality which the Americans prize, and which can manifest itself only in harm and wrong; but if you criticize it, you would surprise and alarm them almost as much as if you attacked the atrocious economic inequality it springs from. (*Letter V*)

The Altrurian—not Howells—brought home to the reader the relationship between uncontrolled individualism in city architecture and crass inequality in economic status.

The littered vacant lots, the hideous billboards on main thoroughfares, the dirty, ill-paved streets, the clanging elevated trains—all these were toned down by the omission of such phrases as "in their competitive system," "in Altrurian eyes" and "of plutocratic society." Though a portion of Howells' diatribe against saloons on Sixth and Seventh avenues was taken over from Aristides' letter and incorporated into his essay, the more plain-spoken sentences, such as the following, were omitted:

> I perceive that as long as there is poverty there must be drunkenness, until the State interferes and sells a man only so much as he can safely drink. Yet, knowing as I do from the daily witness of the press and the courts, that drink is the source of most of the crimes and vices which curse this people, I find the private traffic in alcohol infinitely shocking, and the spectacle of it incredible. (*Letter V*)

In "the old competitive days," Altruria, too, knew the "twin crazes of competition and drunkenness" which are still jealously guarded by Americans as "a chief defense against the advance of Altrurian ideas."

The evils of private ownership of New York stagecoach lines, small shops, dilapidated hovels, empty lots, were clearly observed by the Traveler, who, rather complacently, remarked to Cyril that in Altruria public ownership had wiped out these conditions. Howells, too, was shocked by the chaos he saw about him, behind which stood, in apparently unbroken ranks, the individual owners who did not assume public responsibility. The fact that Howells himself at this time bought and sold many houses, in Boston, New York, and on Long Island,[10] perhaps influenced his decision to delete the following paragraph from the Altrurian's letter when he adapted it for his essay:

> To the Altrurian public the selfishness of a man willing idly to benefit by the industry and energy of others in giving value to his possessions would be unimaginable. Yet this is so common here that it is accepted and honored as a proof of business sagacity; and the man who knows how to hold onto his land, until the very moment when it can enrich him most, though he has neither plowed nor sown it, or laid the foundation of a human dwelling upon it, is honored as a longheaded and solid citizen, who deserves well of his neighbors. (*Letter V*)

Though Howells certainly was not the sort of "solid citizen" he described, he was, through his own experience, deeply interested in the relationship between private ownership of city property and civic responsibility. But disturbed though he might have been by the chaotic conditions he observed around him in New York, Howells continued to live in a "plutocratic society," to draw a salary from Harper & Brothers, and to struggle with his own conflicts.

The distress of mind which accompanied this running argument between Howells and his alter ego, the Altrurian, was evidently too painful to him, for, after adapting Aristides' Letters III, IV, and V for *Impressions and Experiences*, Howells laid the remaining six letters aside and wrote no more on the subject of Altruria for more than thirteen years.

As the century drew to a close, Howells' hope for "the fulfillment of our mission to mankind" waned, and the very word "Altruria" dropped for a time from his vocabulary. To him it seemed that "the present welter of wealth and corpulent expansion" had extinguished "the true American life," and that we stood "gasping in a tide of glory and affluence that may soon or late close over the old American dream forever." [11]

Something of the vehemence of his feeling of the plight of the country at the turn of the century is to be found in an address delivered by Howells on February 28, 1900, before the Twentieth Century Club in Boston, on the subject of "Liberty and Equality." The *Boston Journal* of March 1, 1900, reported that Howells spoke in a monotone for an hour, rarely lifting his eyes from his manuscript, and using no gestures whatever. At the close of his address "he was vociferously applauded." The heading over two columns of the article read, "The Poor vs. the Rich," and though it was essentially the same subject he had treated in all of his Altrurian essays, the word "Altruria" never occured in the address as reported in the *Journal*. The ideas, however, were familiar enough: from "the liberty of Rome, the freedom of Athens and the socialism of Sparta," he said, we gained our concepts of civil liberties. But the pagan world still held to the belief in slavery, and hence represented only a stage in our development. "We must not imagine our state perfect so long as there is one oppressed man in it"; the very notion of equality is meaningless unless accompanied by that of brotherhood. "We say we must change human nature if we want human brotherhood. We really mean that we must change human conditions, and that is quite possible." Not only did Howells make no reference to Altruria in his speech, but he also omitted all allusions to Christianity, though the address was delivered on Ash Wednesday and though he was clearly "preaching" to the audience that packed to overflowing the hall of the Boston University Law School.

Several years later Howells' thoughts returned again to

the remote land of Altruria, where better conditions were supposed to prevail. In 1907, he collected the remaining six "Letters" written for *The Cosmopolitan* in 1894, and edited them to become Part First of *Through the Eye of the Needle*, to which he added an Introduction and a Part Second, written especially for that book. Part First reappeared with few changes, other than the omission of several detailed and rather bitter pages describing the gluttony of New Yorkers in the midst of abject poverty.[12] Except for this one section deleted from Letter IX, the views expressed by the Altrurian in Letters VI to XI were more limited in range than those which appeared in the 1890's. Concerned as they were with descriptions of apartments in a large American city, with the servant problems of New Yorkers, the evening gowns and full-dress suits of the plutocracy, the heavy dinners they served one another, and the drinking and smoking that followed before the gentlemen joined the ladies, one suspects that these letters were more suitable to Harper & Brothers, in 1907, than to *The Cosmopolitan*, in 1894. One has only to turn to Henry Mills Alden's letter to Howells, of September 14, 1888,[13] to see that *The Cosmopolitan* letters included in *Through the Eye of the Needle* were precisely the "feuilleton" that Alden had suggested Howells' sympathy and "altruism" could produce, with "the presentation of the life of our great metropolis" as the subject. "Such a series by Howells would command the interest of all classes, afford food for reflection and conversation in society, and would be largely quoted," he had written. Curiously enough, however, when Howells sought a title for this second Altrurian volume, he chose—perhaps by coincidence—one used by Walker in *The Church and Poverty* in 1891, when these questions seemed to Howells, as well as to Walker, urgently in need of an answer. "How many can be found," Walker had demanded,

who seriously construe the injunction that if struck on one cheek we should turn the other, any more than you can find anyone to-day who will tell you other than that the difficulty about a rich man's entering the kingdom of heaven being likened to a camel's passing through the eye of a needle is purely a matter of speech.[14]

In the Introduction to *Through the Eye of the Needle*, Howells reminded his readers of the fact that Aristides Homos had visited the United States in 1892; that he had been the guest of "a well-known man of letters" at a mountain hotel during the summer before his winter in New York; that in the autumn of the following year he had spent a few days in Chicago, afterwards coming to New York, where he had stayed "until he sailed rather suddenly, for Altruria, taking the circuitous route by which he came." His letters to a friend in his own country, said Howells, with urbane aloofness, were here presented in Part First. Disclaiming all responsibility for the views expressed, Howells seemed to assume again the role of Mr. Twelvemough as a convenient screen, perhaps, to his underlying satire. The letters, he wrote, showed that Aristides was "entangled in his social sophistries regarding all the competitive civilizations." Furthermore,

he cannot apparently do full justice to the superior heroism of charity and self-sacrifice as practised in countries where people live *upon* each other as Americans do, instead of *for* each other as the Altrurians do; but he has some glimmerings of the beauty of our living, and he has undoubtedly the wish to be fair to our ideals. He is unable to value our devotion to the spirit of Christianity amid the practices which seem to deny it; but he evidently wishes to recognise the possibility of such a thing.

What Howells ironically called "social sophistries" in 1907, he had permitted Homos to state directly and forcibly to Cyril in 1893. "Of course," he wrote then,

no Altrurian would think America a civilized country, though many Americans are as truly civilized as ourselves. We should not think it a democratic country, though many Americans are really democrats, and they are all proud of their republican form of government, though it is now little but a form. Far less should we think it a Christian country, though it abounds in good people, who love one another, and lead lives of continual self-sacrifice. (*Letter I*)

Aristides had found that his New York friends were alarmed when he told them that people in Altruria were not motivated by self-interest, for Americans "have so long been accustomed to live *upon* one another that they cannot imagine living *for* one another; in fact, they consider self-interest a very good thing. As for Christ's coming to do away with the old pagan economics as well as the old pagan ethics, they hoot at the notion." At present, Aristides had written at the outset of the crash of 1893, "the cyclone is financial." Though there were no violent outbreaks in the economic world, he had believed that Americans stood on the brink of financial ruin without realizing their danger. The solution lay, Homos had said in "Altrurianizing" both the banks and the industries of the country, "for the sake of the common good as well as the personal good." [15]

When the Altrurian had made his first visit, the United States was experiencing the great economic depression that lasted from 1894 to 1898, Howells reminded his readers of 1907, who again were on the verge of a financial crash. Though bad times had always followed good times, Howells ironically assured his twentieth-century readers, "we have long been enjoying a Golden Age, or Age on a Gold Basis," and "it stands to reason that our present prosperity will never be followed by a period of adversity." Were the Traveler to return in the present era of prosperity, he would see that conditions were entirely changed. Howells, however, did not then mention the "condition" described by the Altrurian in 1892—the workingmen "seated on piles of rubbish in the street with their dinner pails between their knees," "the great heap of offal" daily dumped into vessels and carried out to sea "so that not even the swine may eat of it," the throngs of "hungering men and women and children, who never know what it is to have quite enough." [16] These passages, and others like them, Howells deleted from the "Letters" when he re-edited them for publication by Harper & Brothers in 1907.

What remained of Howells' Altrurian dream of America when he wrote *Through the Eye of the Needle*? Though certainly toned down, the essential idea was still expressed, that our civilization, unless it found its way back to an earlier America, based on Christian-classical beliefs, would eventually be overwhelmed by its own selfish prosperity. In 1894, the Altrurian had considered his American sojourn "a passionate disappointment from first to last . . . a grief which I cannot express." In a similar mood Howells had viewed his country at that time, when he, too, feared "a wild revolt of the poor against the rich." Howells, in his Introduction to *Through the Eye of the Needle*, reviewed the Altrurian's conclusion with an irony which one might call bitter were his comments less humorously worded. "After the Spanish War," he remarked,

Providence marked the divine approval of our victory in that contest by renewing in unexampled measure the prosperity of the Republic. With the downfall of the trusts, and the release of our industrial and commercial forces to unrestricted activity, the condition of every form of labor has been immeasurably improved, and it is now united with capital in bonds of the closest affection.

As a result of the "bonds" of capital and labor, all the minor annoyances of New York living had miraculously disappeared. Indeed, were the Altrurian to return in the prosperous new century, he might be moved to alter his "rash conclusion" as to the wickedness of "the accumulation of money . . . this heaping up of riches . . . which he might not now so totally condemn." For behold, in the "brave new world" of 1907 all was changed:

The trolleys now pass unheard; the elevated train glides by overhead with only a modulated murmur; the subway is a retreat fit for meditation and prayer, where the passenger can possess his soul in a peace to be found nowhere else; the automobile, which was unknown in the day of the Altrurian Emissary, whirs softly through the most crowded thoroughfare, far below the speed limit, with a sigh of gentle satisfaction in its own harmlessness, and, "like the sweet South, taking and giving odor." The streets that he saw so filthy and unkempt in 1893 are now at least as clean as they are quiet.

Furthermore, millionaires spread their blessings to all with no thought of public acknowledgment; businessmen read books; fashionable ladies had solved the servant problem by learning "how to use their helpers"; New York children played happily in fountain-splashed courtyards; tenement houses had become model apartments, and (usually) the tenants were able to pay their rent. Evictions had become so rare that, if one should now take a walk on a cold winter night through one of "the poorer quarters of the town," one would probably not see more than "half a dozen cases of families set out on the sidewalk with their household goods about them." Moreover, "the general decay of snobbishness among us" was noticeable; it was now not unusual to meet interesting and gifted people even at "the table of our highest social leaders," who had quite given up their "Europeanized" manners and had even made progress in "Americanizing" the Europeans.

After reading Howells' satiric Introduction [17]—one can hardly call it "gentle"—one realizes that he still shared in 1907 the views of "the doctrinaire Altrurian," as to the essential "illogicallity of American life." As Homos insisted to Cyril, and as Howells repeated:

logically, the Americans should be what the Altrurians are, since their polity embodies our belief that all men are born equal, with the right to life, liberty, and the pursuit of happiness.

However, he pointed out, Americans were not logical; they still clung to the ideals of Europe, and held "that men are born socially unequal, and deny them the liberty and happiness which can come from equality alone." [18] They lived under conditions "which oblige every man to look after himself," where "a man cannot be a Christian without remorse; he cannot do a generous action without self-reproach; he cannot be nobly unselfish without the fear of being a fool" [19]—or, what is worse, an Altrurian.

NOTES

1. Letter III, "Letters From an Altrurian Traveler," *The Cosmopolitan*, XVI (January, 1894), 259–263. *Letters*, pp. 35–38.
   The first five pages of this third letter in the series were not

reprinted when Howells edited this letter to form the essay, "Glimpses of Central Park" in *Impressions and Experiences* (1896).

2. Letter IV, dated October 30, 1893, appeared in *The Cosmopolitan*, XVI (February, 1894), 415–425. Letter V, dated November, 1893, may be found in the same volume of *The Cosmopolitan*, XVI (March, 1894), 558–567. *Letters*, 54–76.

3. That Howells, half playfully, thought of himself as the Altrurian, is suggested by the signature he affixed to a letter to his daughter Mildred on November 5, 1915, when he signed himself "Your affectionate father, Hywel Altruria," *Life in Letters*, II, 353.

4. Letter III was entitled "A Bit of Altruria in New York," when it appeared in *The Cosmopolitan*, XVI (January, 1894), 276.

5. The ideas expressed in this paragraph were expanded by Howells over a year later in "Equality as the Basis of Good Society," *Century*, LI (November, 1895), 63–67.

6. Letter IV was entitled, in *The Cosmopolitan*, "Aspects and Impressions of a Plutocratic City"; Letter V was called "Plutocratic Contrasts and Contradictions."

7. *The World of Chance* (1893), embodying many of these ideas, appeared in *Harper's* between March and November, 1892.

8. Paragraphs from Letter V, on drinking in New York, are deleted (See *The Cosmopolitan*, XVI, 564–565. *Letters*, pp. 71–72). Here Howells substituted an extensive section from Letter IX, *The Cosmopolitan*, XVII (July, 1894), 352–353. *Letters*, pp. 106–107. These paragraphs from Letter IX will be found, with few changes, in "New York Streets," *Impressions and Experiences*, pp. 269–272.

9. 40 West Fifty-ninth Street. This building is now gone, as is also the old Plaza where the Altrurian probably stayed. The new Plaza, now standing, was built on the same site in 1907. For Howells' comment on what he saw from his window, see *American Authors and Their Homes*, edited by Francis Whiting Halsey, 1902, pp. 103–104.

10. Four homes passed through Howells' hands during his fifteen years in Boston. When his estate was settled, he owned two houses in New York City, 259 West Eighty-fifth Street and 314 West Eighty-second Street, having probably transferred to his son a third New York house, 38 East Seventy-third Street. After Howells' death, his heirs continued to occupy the

home in Kittery, Maine. During his life he owned, for a short time, a home at Far Rockaway, Long Island, and another in York, Maine, as well as a co-operative apartment in New York City.

11. "Editor's Easy Chair," *Harper's*, CIII (August, 1901), 493. See also "The Limitations of Irony," *Harper's Weekly*, XLVI (February 1, 1902), 133.

12. When Howells considered Letter IX for Section XVII of *Through the Eye of the Needle*, he found that he had already used the first portion of the Letter in "New York Streets." Several more pages of this "Letter" seemed inappropriate to him when he edited it for inclusion in his new book in 1907. (See *The Cosmopolitan*, XVII, 353–356. *Letters*, pp. 107–108.)

13. See Chapter 1 of this book.

14. See Howells' discussion of the story of the rich man and "a needle's eye" in "Are the Americans Bible Readers?" *Literature*, n.s. I, No. 25 (June 30, 1899), 585–586.

15. *The Cosmopolitan*, XVI (November, 1893), 110–112. *Letters*, pp. 13–15.

16. *The Cosmopolitan*, XVII (June, 1894), 353–355. *Letters*, pp. 107–109.

17. Apparently, Howells' irony was not recognized as such when *The Needle* appeared in 1907. See A. Schade van Westrum, "Altruria Once More," *The Bookman*, XXV (June, 1907), 434–435.

18. *Through the Eye of the Needle*, pp. 24–25.

19. *Idem.*, Section I, p. 4. Though Howells effectively veiled his language when he returned to his Altrurian fantasy in *Through the Eye of the Needle*, he did not hesitate to support Eugene V. Debs as presidential candidate for the Socialist party in 1906. Morris Hillquit, in *Loose Leaves From a Busy Life* (1934), pp. 116–117, wrote: "Support of the Socialist candidates in the district came from persons in high places in the literary and academic worlds. We were particularly proud of the endorsement of William D. Howells, the dean of American letters, then in his sixty-ninth year, who sent us a warm letter of encouragement with a campaign contribution."

Epilogue

Before Howells brought his "Letters From an Altrurian Traveller" to a close in 1894, he, of course, had to make good his promise of "a romance." Through Mrs. Makely, the Altrurian was introduced [1] to the beautiful, wealthy widow, Mrs. Eveleth Strange, who lived with her mother in an East-side mansion, bequeathed to her by her deceased husband. It soon appeared that the heroine—like Annie Kilburn before her [2]—was baffled by the problem of how to help the poor with her riches, without giving too much of herself. The Altrurian, to whom she unburdened her heart, knew the answer, for he, like Howells, was a Christian Socialist. He realized that, in terms both of Christianity and democracy, one must practice brotherly love and forget the distinctions between rich and poor, servant and master. If one were to save one's own soul, as well as that of society, he said to Eveleth, "it must be in the spirit of the First Altrurian":

We must come poor to the poor; we must not try to win any one, save through his heart and conscience; we must be as simple and humble as the least of those that Christ bade follow Him.

Naturally enough, these fervent conversations between the Altrurian (who turned out to be a bachelor of thirty-five) and Eveleth led to the "romance" every reader of Howells had learned to expect. After a pleasant New York winter of dinner parties, balls, receptions, and afternoon teas, the two announced their engagement. Here the trouble began, for it slowly dawned on Eveleth that the Altrurian really believed the ideas he so freely expresses—that, in fact, he saw no reason why his bride should not give up her handsome house, her splendid carriages, and her bank account, and return with him to Altruria, there to stay. "You must choose," he said, "between me and your money; no; not me!—but between love and your money. You cannot keep both." Eveleth's argument, that "Tolstoy himself doesn't destroy his money, though he wants other people to," fell on deaf ears. When Eveleth fully grasped the Altrurian's meaning, she responded to the challenge, as a romantic heroine must, by casting herself on her lover's bosom and stopping his mouth "with an impassioned kiss." [3]

However, the Eye of the Needle was too narrow. A night of restless tossing restored Eveleth to her senses; she wrote a brief note to Aristides, which caused him to reel as he read it. Eveleth at last admitted that she was, indeed, the creature of her environment and, therefore, must renounce her lover rather than her fortune. Thus Howells, in 1894, made it clear that altrurianism cannot wed materialism; the gulf between them is impassable. For almost fourteen years this unromantic ending remained the conclusion to the brief flirtation between an Altrurian Traveler and an American heiress.

When Howells, in 1907, picked up the threads of his story, he hastened to inform the reader that Part Second of *Through the Eye of the Needle* was "by another hand," and one which was not to be trusted "since it is a woman's hand and not to be credited with the firm and unerring touch of a man's." The letters, fifteen in number, were ostensibly written by Eveleth Strange (now Mrs. Homos) from her home in Altruria to her New York friend, Mrs. Makely. This account of Altruria, the editor warned in the Introduction, "can by no means have the sociological value" of Homos' earlier record, though it does describe conditions "which some of our dreamers would consider ideal." Part Second, which we are here considering as one essay, was the reflection of Eveleth's "desultory and imperfect glimpses of a civilization fundamentally alien to her own, such as would attract an enthusiastic nature."

Howells himself was, of course, the "dreamer" whose "enthusiastic nature" still lured him to meditate upon Altruria, in spite of the disillusioning years which intervened between Part First and Part Second of his later Altrurian Romance. As in 1893, so in 1907, America stood on the edge of a "financial cyclone," the full force of which was soon to be felt in all circles. Both *The Traveler* and *The Needle* appeared a few months before an actual crash and a depression in this country. In these two books, Howells clearly indicated what seemed to him the remedy—a return to the concepts of civil liberties set forth in the Declaration of Independence, which came originally from Palestine by way of Greece and had to do with the redemption of the individual in terms of brotherhood. The word which Howells found to express this thought was "altruism." But the Spanish War, the gold controversy, the growth of the railroads, the birth of the steel corporation, the rise of immigrations—all these social changes, and many more, brought with them problems which left the aging Howells less willing to dogmatize. He felt, indeed, "a sort of misgiving as to the reality of things seen and heard" by Eveleth Strange, as she described them in her letters home from Altruria—which, in 1907, seemed to have moved even further away from America. "It is a pity," the weary editor remarked, that "a more absolute conclusion" cannot be derived from this "lively lady's knowledge of the ideal country of her adoption," that sunny land which is at once reminiscent of our earlier America and akin to our vision of Greece. Her very name, "Eveleth Strange," suggested that his heroine was, from the beginning, Eve in search of a lost Paradise, from which she had wandered into a strange world (she was Miss Gray before her marriage); she had sipped of the River of Lethe, or Oblivion, and could no longer feel sure of either world. "Eveleth" was Eve Asleep.

Eveleth Homos, in her letters to Dorothea Makely, was not quite sure where Altruria was to be found on the map, whether it was perhaps nearer to Australia than to Greece.[4] She was certain, however, that the country was beautiful, the sky clear, and the water blue. In Altruria, Eveleth wrote her friend, she dressed in "pretty, classic fashions," [5] like a character in a Greek play at Harvard, and shared in the daily work in the fields and vineyards, as well as in the dancing and the singing of these people who enjoyed "life, liberty and the pursuit of happiness." She also enjoyed the public meetings held in "the principal edifice, marble and classic and tasteful," called the temple,[6] where discussions on many subjects were held by the assembled men and women. Not infrequently "the American situation" came up for consideration, and then Aristides was called upon to explain the "gigantic joke" implicit in the American concepts of patriotism, war, education, labor, and justice. Eveleth, listening to his descriptions of the remote barbarians of North America, was moved to wonder whether her native land was simply a bad dream, or Altruria itself only a beautiful one, and her husband, Aristides, a myth—"though a thoroughly *good* myth." The reader, for his part, had every right to conclude that Eveleth might at any moment awake from her dream and find herself again in her New York mansion. Though Howells did not rouse his heroine from her pleasant slumbers, he left one with the impression that only in dreams could an American heiress pass through the Eye of the Needle, and make her home in a land where social customs are marked by Greek simplicity and where selfishness is replaced by Christian love.

The summer before Howells wrote Part II of *Through the Eye of the Needle* he journeyed from Kittery Point to Cambridge to see *Agamemnon* performed in the open air by Harvard students. In spite of overcast skies and inter-mittent drizzle, Aeschylus' play "was one of the most beau-tiful things that could be imagined, and perfectly done," Howells wrote his sister the next day. "Half the time we sat under umbrellas, but the colors of the costumes on the green grass, and the sonorous grandeur of the language, with the students' fine acting of the noble tragedy, made us forget the wet." [7]

The beauty of the Greek world, never far from How-ells' imagination, was felt throughout Mrs. Homos' descrip-tions of Altruria in her letters to Mrs. Makely; for the Altrurian's wife was the character through whom Howells made his final comment on the civilization on which he had brooded since, as a boy, he had read Goldsmith's *History of Greece.* Something of the perennial charm and freshness of existence seemed to Howells to linger about the antique world; it still held a meaning, for "the world itself is new to every generation; and under the hoary ashes of antiquity the latest of the moderns feels the appeal of a kindred life that once was." [8] The American notion of the Greeks was necessarily "of the mind" and erroneous, Howells admitted, but it recognized with certainty that the Greeks "made existence on the earth here a fine art," [9] and whenever a writer or artist "succeeds in representing life, he is seen to have something Greek; that is something true, something free, something beautiful, something novel, something temperate." [10]

Howells wrote the second part of *Through the Eye of the Needle* in 1907, and though he found it rather more difficult to believe in the power of "human nature" to live permanently in Altruria than when he wrote the first Altrurian essays in the 1890's, his vision essentially "remained unchanged through every change of time and place." In the summer of 1909 Howells began preparing the Library Edition of his works; he then proposed to put together in one volume *A Traveler From Altruria* and *Through the Eye of the Needle,* for these two books seemed to him to be "of one blood" and "of the same generation and born of the same abiding conviction": that emulation, rather than competition, is the only solution of our economic problems.[11] The volume was never published, though the Preface was written in the made-over barn, called "the Barnbury," attached to his summer home at Kittery Point.

Howells, then aged 75, was so imbued with his vision of a Greco-Christian Altruria, tinged with socialism, that he was delighted to "preach" on the subject in the white colonial church which still stands across the road from the Howells home. "What do you think of my preaching yesterday in the church here?" he wrote his wife; "Their 'supply' didn't come and the crowd got round and pleaded with me so to speak or read, that I raced over to the Barnbury, got the *Trav. from Altruria,* and gave 'em a good dose of socialism. They liked it so well that they all shook hands and thankt me. Marthy reported later that it was the greatest hit ever known in K.P." [12] Hesitant as Howells was as a speaker, the words came freely—no doubt, more to the surprise of the speaker than the congregation.

For over twenty years, first through the Altrurian and then through the Altrurian's wife, Howells had "preached" to the country, for he feared that plutocratic America was pursuing a course leading away from, rather than toward, the ideals of Altruria, which were essentially those of our founding fathers.

"But what proof shall I give you," Aristides asked in despair, "that there is such a land as Altruria?" The answer given by Howells remained the same throughout all of the Altrurian papers, though the vehemence with which he delivered it varied: "If the darkness implies the day, America must imply Altruria." For the sake of the doubter, the Altrurian added,

> In what way do I seem false, or mad, except that I claim to be the citizen of a country where people love one another as the first Christians did? [13]

Just as Aristides claimed that Christianity was the source of his social beliefs, though his native land lay very near to Greece, so Howells recognized his—and his country's—allegiance to these two traditions in his dream of an Altrurian America. Through Aristides, Howells was able to imagine "a prophecy of the truer state" which, he believed, "America is destined yet to see established." [14]

NOTES

1. See Letter VIII. *The Cosmopolitan*, XVII (June, 1894), 221–228; *Letters*, pp. 98–105. This Letter became Sections XIV, XV, and XVI, Part First, of *Through the Eye of the Needle*.
2. *Annie Kilburn*, 1888.
3. *The Cosmopolitan*, XVII (October, 1894), 617–618; *Letters*, pp. 126–127.
4. Louis J. Budd, in "Altruism Arrives in America," *op. cit.*, points out that Howells here draws on the latest news about Australia. Footnote 22, p. 48.
5. *Through the Eye of the Needle*, p. 137.
6. *Idem.*, pp. 158–159.
7. *Life in Letters*, II, 225.
8. "The Editor's Study," *Harper's*, LXXXIV (January, 1892), 319.
9. *Idem.*, CXIV (December, 1906), 155.
10. *Idem.*, LXXXII (April, 1891), 803.
11. "Howells's Unpublished Prefaces," *op. cit.*, pp. 589–590.
12. *Life in Letters*, II, 266.
13. *Through the Eye of the Needle*, p. 104.
14. Letter III, *The Cosmopolitan*, XVI (January, 1894), 263; *Letters*, p. 39.

Index